Praise For

"As someone who h... ..., ... to me. I'm not talking about an awakening with pomp and circumstance, but something more simple, beautiful, and powerful. PC has always been a guiding force in my life, and this incredibly powerful book is no different."
—Kyle Lacy, 3x Author and National Speaker

"*Beneath Broken Machines* is a cup of cold water to a dry, parched, and weary soul. In ministry, it is easy to portray that I ONCE was lost...but now I've got it all together. PC writes this book with humility and openness, which gives permission to confess that your machine is broken as well."
—Travis Osborne, Pastor at Vintage Faith Church in Santa Cruz, CA

"PC speaks with a sense of honesty and humility about our brokenness. His book brings refreshment resulting from our openness to call sin 'sin.' He challenges us to confess or admit the nature of our wrongs. This is a good book from a humble man. Read it!"
—Dr. Patrick Blewett, Dean of A.W. Tozer Theological Seminary

"*Beneath Broken Machines* separates what we DO from who we ARE and invites a generation that is fleeing the church back to community and fellowship...and ultimately, back to the great love of their Papa."
—Lisa Pay, Professor of Social Work at Anderson University

BENEATH BROKEN MACHINES

Reviving Trust in the Heart of the Gospel

PC WALKER

WestBow Press
A DIVISION OF THOMAS NELSON
& ZONDERVAN

Copyright © 2016 PC Walker.

All rights reserved. No part of this book may be used or reproduced by any means, graphic, electronic, or mechanical, including photocopying, recording, taping or by any information storage retrieval system without the written permission of the author except in the case of brief quotations embodied in critical articles and reviews.

This book is a work of non-fiction. Unless otherwise noted, the author and the publisher make no explicit guarantees as to the accuracy of the information contained in this book and in some cases, names of people and places have been altered to protect their privacy.

Scripture quotations are from The Holy Bible, English Standard Version® (ESV®), copyright © 2001 by Crossway, a publishing ministry of Good News Publishers. Used by permission. All rights reserved.

WestBow Press books may be ordered through booksellers or by contacting:

WestBow Press
A Division of Thomas Nelson & Zondervan
1663 Liberty Drive
Bloomington, IN 47403
www.westbowpress.com
1 (866) 928-1240

Because of the dynamic nature of the Internet, any web addresses or links contained in this book may have changed since publication and may no longer be valid. The views expressed in this work are solely those of the author and do not necessarily reflect the views of the publisher, and the publisher hereby disclaims any responsibility for them.

Any people depicted in stock imagery provided by Thinkstock are models, and such images are being used for illustrative purposes only. Certain stock imagery © Thinkstock.

ISBN: 978-1-5127-5975-4 (sc)
ISBN: 978-1-5127-5976-1 (hc)
ISBN: 978-1-5127-5974-7 (e)

Library of Congress Control Number: 2016916714

Print information available on the last page.

WestBow Press rev. date: 10/06/2016

To Tonya,
my wife and most magnificent Gift of Grace

CONTENTS

Foreword *by David Leo Schultz*....................... ix
Foreword *by Ben McDonald* xiii
Acknowledgements................................... xv
Beneath Broken Machines (a poem) xix
Introduction... xxiii

1. Filthy Rags and Gas Station Bathroom......... 1
2. The Well-Oiled Machine 15
3. The Lip of the Grand Canyon 30
4. Your God Is Too Small [another poem].......... 42
5. Walking the Gangly Wire 45
6. Boo Boo Buddies and Daddy, I Love Yous..... 58
7. Faint Shadows and Too Much Light.............. 73
8. The Wobbly and Weak-kneed....................... 89
9. Telescopes To Heaven 105
10. Deeper Senses of Home 118
11. When the Mighty Descend and the
    Lowly Rise 133
12. Step Out Onto Nothing............................... 150

Notes 165

FOREWORD BY DAVID LEO SCHULTZ

PC has a way with words. He always has. When I picture my friend of nearly twenty years I picture an obsessed poet and romantic tucked away in some hole-in-the-wall coffee shop, savoring every drop of the perfectly made coffee while he writes with a vicious fury, trying to capture every nuance he has experienced in his "entanglement" times with God.

I can write a favorable review of this book, not just because his words are calculated and dazzling, but also because I know the scribe behind the words. While he has a way with rhetoric and poetry, behind the rhythms and rhymes is a child who is dazed and confused about the bountiful and awe-inspiring love of God.

If you have a false idea of who God is, PC might say, "Your God is too small for me!" But the God I have witnessed in PC's words, and more importantly, in PC's life, is not too small for me. At times, if not all the time, He is too big for me. He does not let His bigness stand in the way of clobbering me with His love. And he loves spoiling PC.

There is a dramatic difference between knowing God loves you and experiencing His love. PC is one who has stepped into the middle of the thunderstorm of God's love and has lived to tell about it. How do I know? I've seen it!

In the middle of nowhere, somewhere in Mississippi, I have seen PC, on many occasions, a manly man, weep like a baby. He lay behind our poorly made backdrop constructed for our sketch comedy show, which was merely a means to an end: to share the gospel with any and all who were willing to listen. I cannot recall if we said anything to each other. But I do remember us hugging each other. I remember the warmth of that embrace. It was a moment of kindred souls who were simultaneously touched by the divine.

We had both witnessed and experienced the presence of God's love ambushing a small church camp chapel out of nowhere. It was inexplicable. But one thing was clear: it seemed we both had the same thought running through our hearts and minds, and it was shouting, "He really does love us!" I think for both PC and me, and our other ragtag troupe of ragamuffins, we were in awe! And we still are!

With this book, PC runs around the fields of poetry and rhetoric screaming like a "sweaty toothed madman" to come and experience this awe. There is awe of God's love, which is often wild as a "reckless raging fury." I am here to tell you PC is the real deal. He is honest and broken. He is silly and serious. He is both a sinner and a saint. PC has many strengths, but his most powerful weapon is grace.

So I dare you to soak in the poetry and compelling grace that fills these pages. Because if you do, you too might just be ambushed by the grace and love of our great awe-inspiring God. That is what I am excited about! There is a moment when reading this book that you may be ushered into the presence of our loving God. Be careful in that moment. You too will never be the same. I am excited for you in that moment to hear what God has to say to you. For He also has a way with words!

PC, thank you for nearly 20 years of grace-filled friendship. Thank you for the gift of your friendship that has seen me at my best and my worst, but never letting either of those realities restrict you from using your most powerful weapon on me.

>Your fellow ragamuffin,
>David Leo Schultz
>Writer and Director of the films *Ragamuffin* and *Brennan* and author of *Sinners, Saints, and the Furious Love of God*

FOREWORD BY BEN MCDONALD

The world has become so fast-paced, and in no time at all, we realize that the ideal life we thought we were living has become a cold, hardened, hopeless place.

This book is an invitation to hit pause, exit the rat race, and embrace the truth of the human experience as God intended. It paints a broad picture that each individual is a vulnerable child in the hands of a relentlessly loving Father.

This book is a great reminder of why we were created, a must-read for anyone who is feeling lifeless and hopeless.

    Ben McDonald
    Co-Founder and Guitarist for *Sidewalk Prophets*

ACKNOWLEDGEMENTS

This book would never have happened if I were left to my own promptings. So many people have pushed into the clay that has formed the man I am now, and they ought to be known as contributors to a book with this much of my heart attached. I am certain to forget a great number of people, but I would like to thank the following:

- My wife, Tonya, for always and forever being my greatest gift of grace, my partner and lover for 12 years. She is the main impetus to get me moving on actually writing a book without any excuses. She told me if I still have the dream to write, "You are going to have to fight for that dream. There are a lot of important things you continue to make *more* important than the dream God has given you."
- My two daughters, who have been the greatest joys in my life. Bryleigh, my greatest theology professor, and Haddisen, who reminds me to see my world through the eyes of joy and peace.
- My mom, my dad, and Tim and Linda, who have all seen and noticed things in me to call out and never overlook. Also, for the time and love given

to my children, you all are incredible Gagas and Papas, and that is the greatest gift to me.
- Will Hullinger, who has urged me so persistently to write a book. In college, he prayed for a number of friends individually. He remembers God telling him, regarding me, "Don't let him say, 'No!'" That was Will's task for now and into eternity.
- My editor, Sabrina Leroe, who made me fall in love with the phrase "Accept Change". Thank you so much for making me sound so much smarter than I really am. You are the best.
- Every friend who has incessantly demanded that I write a book: Evonne DeSanders, Erin Rohr, David Pepsny, Anthony and Malisa Price, Brandon and Nicole Farmer, Danny and Erin Reynoso, Jesse and Joanna Peterson (Merger), and Justin and Anh Powers.
- Ron Frye, who though we have come to a hurtful disconnection and distance in the later parts of my life, your impact on the man I have become is never to be denied or overlooked. You are the reason I have pursued intimacy with the heart of God.
- Brennan Manning, whose writing has transformed my perspective of Abba, the gospel, and myself in relation to the first two. Save a spot near Abba for me.
- The Color Green, the most irreverent preachers of the gospel I have ever known. David, Kyle, Justin, Shawn, and Randy have been my brothers who sat together many late nights talking about Jesus. We were obsessed with Jesus. We were obsessed with preaching the gospel we barely understood.

I know they are broken men who will not tell me they are praying for me unless they certainly are praying for me. There is no Christian pretense to wade through, no churchy language to sort out, but there is true love that stands sometimes (most of the time) without answers. Those are the friends we all ought to have.

- For every person who listened to my heart for this project and my anxiety over the pieces I knew nothing about (promotion, marketing, launching, artwork, etc.) and said, "You are my friend, PC, and I want in." Thank you, Gabe Wahl, Michael McLaughlin, Jeff Eberhardt, Jason Squires, and Sandra Dimas. I know each of you is worth far more than the nothing I paid you.

- For my different forms of family who have been encouragement, spurs, and bellows to the fire in my heart. Thank you to my families at Jesus Culture of Sacramento, Powerhouse Ministries, A.W. Tozer Theological Seminary, Anderson University, and my small group in rural Elk Grove, CA.

BENEATH BROKEN MACHINES (A POEM)

He told me, "We're very proud of the ministry we have here.
We've worked very hard to build a well-oiled machine."
He went on to describe what I could only assume to be
parts of his machine, and he asked
if I could see myself as a part.
I wish he had not asked.

You see, some people build their faith
like a well-oiled machine. They put in all their efforts
in hopes the machine will produce the right product. Beware
when your faith becomes a well-oiled machine
for machines have no hearts.

And some people build their faith
like a well-oiled machine that keeps breaking down.
They put in all their efforts, and the machine will not produce.
Take courage, my friend, it is still a machine,
and machines have no hearts.

Machines have no need for miracles. They only ask for miracles
and then operate in ways to make miracles unnecessary.
Machines are built with big goals and bigger breakdowns,

and I wish I could write these words in braille
so someone could feel what I am saying;
You don't need God
to build a machine.

But the gospel is for the broken ones
smart enough to know how foolish they are.
It is for those who have tried and found life lacking,
but who are not content to confess that
this is all there is.

It is for those wearied by wondering if our crying hearts
might drown us, but who know our tears
are telescopes to heaven, looking through trembling lenses
for hope and deeper senses of home.

It is for those who do not need church to be
a menagerie of saints, but an emergency room
for sinners. It is for those whose shadows are faint
from finding too much light.

The gospel is for those who will step out onto nothing,
hoping to land on something, because accepting that
you are accepted
is a perception of yourself not everyone can afford.
It is for the wobbly and weak-kneed who have let loose
the luxury
of denying the handout of amazing grace.

It is for those who chose a path,
though straight and narrow is still rugged and beaten.
You are still on the right path!

The gospel is for the phobic confessor who could never match
the projections of the pious, but who knows
perfection is a gangly wire no one could ever walk.

It is for the child who holds that heaven is full of five-year-olds,
sparing themselves the futility of proving themselves
to people who will never speak your language;
Half trust, half boo boos, half "Daddy I love yous."
Three halves make one more than whole.

Do not accept yourself as you should be, but as you are,
because you will never be as you should be.
Quit rinsing your filthy rags in gas station bathrooms
as if hand soap and make-believe
will make them believe you belong.

But you belong.
You belong to a kingdom-belonging people not trying
to be cleaner than they are. You belong!

The gospel is for the sin-soaked and the broken
who are loved and outspoken;
knowing unworthy is not the same as worth*less*.
It is for the paupers who have made peace with their flaws.
It is for those who have prayed in silence
but have never ceased to pray.

The gospel is for you.
Do not, for one second, take your gift for granted.
Make sure your gift is contagious, because while it is yours to have,

it is only valuable in its giving away.
Make sure your every conversation leaves
a sensation of love.

Because this is where the mighty descends and the lowly rises
to comprise what we all crave.
It is standing on the lip of the Grand Canyon with a contagious tour guide
telling you, "Look at *this!* Look at *that!* Look at *this!*"
If the Grand Canyon is only a faint glimpse of God's glory, you have to wonder,
What must *He* be like?

You are not a machine.
You are a child of God with a beating heart.
You are a tour guide to God's love and glory.

INTRODUCTION

I am not a handy person. When anything breaks in my house I am faced with an immediate decision. I have to determine whether this item will be fixed or thrown away. If I cannot find a step-by-step solution on YouTube or get someone else handy enough to help, I am going to throw that machine away. I am not qualified to repair most of my machines.

Most of us build life and faith like a well-oiled machine, but it keeps breaking down. We start to wonder if the machine is "over" and needs thrown away or if we are going to be handy enough to fix all the broken pieces on our own. Machines have no hearts, and yet we operate in ways to make machinery out of our rigid religious efforts and routines. We forget to encounter the heart of Jesus.

The trouble with our faith being a well-oiled machine is that machines break down. We are all broken people, but when the machine breaks we can see the heart, soul, and spirit that lies beneath our broken machines. This is where encounters with the gospel of Jesus really take place.

I carry a small obsession in my life. I have wanted a Volkswagen Vanagon with a pop-up camper tent on top for years. I hold on to hope for one day being blessed with this gift. My father-in-law has a beautiful 1968 cherry red VW Bug he has restored to great beauty. He is a man of numerous trades and talents. When he discovered my desire for a VW, he was excited. He also said, "You realize, when you buy a Volkswagen, you are buying a project? If you are okay with that, I can help you get the right tools to keep in your van at all times for *when* you break down."

No matter how beautiful your manufactured machine of faith appears, it will break at some point. There will be moments when life breaks it down; many Christians have found themselves alongside the fragmented pieces of the religious machine they tried to maintain. They have attended church regularly and listened to enlightening sermons for years. They have done all they could to remain good people with better morals than their coworkers. They can recite all the right answers at just the right time. They have completed every Bible reading plan they have ever started, and the *ichthus* sticker on the back of their car has never faded in the hot sun. Once their machine began to break under the weight of different life circumstances, they found themselves wondering, "What else does God want from me?"

They have missed the heart of Jesus Christ as revealed in His grace and love. We have missed the tools we find in the gospel. This book is for the person whose machine is broken. It is for the one who needs to be reminded of the heart below the machine. The gospel screams of a love that will rattle all of your neatly arranged designs. The gospel is saturated with life, love, and grace. These are not machine parts for you to maintain; they are heart experiences you embrace and accept.

This book is the toolbox you ought to keep with you at all times for *when* the machinery you have built breaks down. If you read this book, and out of disappointment, throw it away (or delete it, if you have the digital version), it would be the greatest outcome I could have expected from you. I do not know how anyone can write a book without feeling like an imposter. Every one of these pages is filled with advice I barely know how to give, and I have only intermittently lived it out in my own life. Still, you will find here pages full of words that sound very confident.

If my goal were to do what everyone says I ought to: "Write what you know," you would find nothing interesting in these pages (You still may not!), because what I know would make for a terrible book. This is not a collection of the things I know; it is a collection of the things I want and need to read myself. I hope you find in these pages something you need.

      PC Walker
      Sacramento, CA

FILTHY RAGS AND GAS STATION BATHROOMS

THE LIFE OF faith is made up of a series of reality checks we would like to avoid, but there is no life in our spirituality when we avoid these experiences. When we walk away from these moments, we push our spirituality off a cliff to its death because we would rather give up our spirituality than to sacrifice a faith lived on our own terms.

Jesus said the truly blessed ones are the ones who know they are spiritually poor. I am on the verge of something great the moment I come to terms with my spiritual poverty. When I come to terms with the reality that I am not the center of the universe, I find spiritual growth. The threshold of real spiritual life is where I accept the fact I am relentlessly selfish, broken, and torn down. The gospel is only embraced by those who know they need it.

The company Jesus kept gives us a clear picture of the type of person I want to become. He had compassion for the failures and the marginalized. He spent a lopsided amount of time with dregs of society, but his love was not exclusive in this way. He also gave compassion to the mighty ones in the culture. He could give love to both because he knew they all belong to God. The gospel is not only for the financially poor and the politically oppressed, but it is for all those who are rich enough with grace to recognize their own poverty of heart.

Jesus was magnetized to the unappealing. He had an odd desire for the unwanted. He eliminated any dividing line between the affluent and the average. His attraction is made clear in his invitation to all who sweat and are overloaded: "Come to me, and I will give you rest" (Matt. 11:28). It sounds so great! But why is it so hard to do?

We all have moments when our spirit could use a rest. We all have moments when our hearts have been bested by our sin, our struggles, and the general beating life has to offer. We all have moments when we feel attacked by our past, held down by our present, and fearful of our future. Some of us live weary and heavy-laden, and this passage sounds like amazing freedom. Our hearts jump at the possibility. But we remain weary, and rest remains a possibility, never a reality. Why is it so hard to actually come to Jesus for rest?

First, it is humiliating. We feel like peasants before God, utterly unworthy of the rest He offers. We see ourselves in the reality of our filth. We look at our sin and our predicament, and it paralyzes us. We stay back and grovel just outside Jesus' presence because we know we are unworthy, but we have convinced ourselves that we are *worthless*. There is a difference. We stay just outside Jesus' open arms, which offer our weary hearts rest, because we fear rejection. We fear ourselves to be too filthy, too broken, and too far gone.

Still, Jesus calls out to you, "Come to me." He knows your predicament. He sees your filth. He realizes what has worn you down and deteriorated your heart, and He still invites you to come. It is only hard to come to Jesus for rest because we would rather stay in sorrow than to accept God's invitation to a grace and love that says, "I know you are weary, filthy, and broken, but I love you. Please come to me, and I will love all that torment out of you."

This invitation was illustrated in an interaction I had with a homeless man named Arliss. As Tonya and I walked the cold streets of Chicago, a man approached us with showerless days layered upon him. When I refused him change, I asked if I could get him something else. He asked for a hot cup of coffee. That would not be denied him. I asked him to join us inside, but Arliss told me, "They ain't gonna let me in there, man!"

"Why not?" I pretended.

"They don't serve homeless people in there."

"Oh," I said, "I'm not homeless, and I'm paying for it. They will serve me."

He reluctantly accepted my invitation, gathered himself, and removed his hat to enter the building. He had more manners than many of us would have had—I have never removed my hat when entering a building. Tonya and I walked in normally, and he joined us, with hesitance and shyness. We were not 10 feet in the door when the barista spoke up from behind the bar. Clearing her throat loudly, she addressed Arliss, "Um...sir?"

Arliss' head shot up to attention and caught the barista's eye.

"You need to leave." She motioned toward the door like an owner disciplines a disobedient dog.

Arliss immediately lost his demeanor. He lowered his head apologetically and slowly turned to walk out. He must have been thinking, "I told you, man! Why did you ask me to do this? I told you this would happen."

I stood frozen for a second before I responded to the barista with an assured poise.

"No, no, no, ma'am. He's with me. He's a paying customer."

I asked Arliss to stay with me.

The barista replied with silence and a wry wrinkle of her mouth. She shook her head but reluctantly conceded.

We are only concerned with how filthy we are when we are in the presence of something or someone who is cleaner. Arliss had no concern for how filthy he was. He was normal on the street. He would sit there all day with a smile if I had never asked him in for coffee. Arliss did not realize how filthy he was until he was inside a clean business establishment he was never allowed into before.

Sometimes I wonder whether I made the right choice. Should I have just gone in to get him a cup of coffee and brought it out to him? I am not sure that would have been any better.

But you should have seen his face when I stood in the gap between clean and filthy and said, "No! He's with me." You should have seen his face when he realized someone saw him as clean and worthy of dignity, hope, and love, despite his clothes. I imagine it was the same as Isaiah's face when the angel bridged the gap between clean and filthy, and declared, "Your guilt is taken away, and your sin atoned for" (Is. 6:7). You should see your face when you acknowledge the difference between unworthy and worthless, and accept your need for a savior.

Who is this Jesus to you? He has to first be Savior and Lord before He can be Teacher. Anyone who begins with Jesus as only a good Teacher would remain hopeless in the gospel, because not even the best pupil or disciple could really accomplish His teachings. You need Jesus, first, to be your Savior and Lord. It is the only way to begin with the necessary insight that you cannot accomplish even a portion of His teaching. Are you poor enough in spirit to know your need for rescue from an undeserving and incapable condition?

This poverty of heart instantly creates community. People who realize their true poor spirit know they cannot be as self-sufficient as they had always hoped. It is in a creative interdependency that the mystery of life unfolds itself a lot more.[1]

Only after this realization can you look with confidence upon any of Jesus' teaching for your life as a follower. Without His rescue, I remain in despair all the days of my life when I compare those days to the life He actually teaches me to live. I will never measure up without His rescue.

I am saved, controlled, and covered by His Spirit in those places I wish I could but could never accomplish on my own. If I begin with my poor and humble need, Jesus says I am blessed (Matthew 5). You will be happy when you begin with a humble understanding that you could not accomplish even half of His teaching if not for His Spirit and salvation in your core.

The gospel of Jesus belongs to people who are not trying to be cleaner than they are. They are not trying to rinse their filthy rags in gas station bathrooms with all their furious efforts at calling attention to how good they look on the outside. The gospel of Jesus belongs to people for whom there is no need to be concerned with whether or not they will get accolades for their stellar behavior. They realize their striving for perfectionism is as narcissistic as any overt braggart. "The lostness of the resentful 'saint' is so hard to reach precisely because it is so closely wedded to the desire to be good and virtuous."[2] People who know the gospel in their hearts know they cannot, nor do they have to, know all the right answers at all the right times.

Jesus told us to become like little children, and by this He means for us to learn how to be present with the Father in the moment (Lk.18:15-17). Paul knew a great deal of what it meant to become like little children when he said, "All I can say is that I forget the past and I strain ahead for what is still to come" (Phil. 3:13). He strains ahead without wallowing in the past. Paul accepts himself as being of little account.

Children were the lowest of the low in the society at the time of Paul's writing; they were among the societal stratification of prostitutes, tax collectors, and those plagued by other societal ills. But children do not realize that they are held in such low esteem. Not restrained or affected by the disdain of society, they simply came to Jesus with a desire to be near to Him, and Jesus tells us, "You are to come to me in this way." He takes pleasure in seeing those who will come close to Him, not because they deserve to, but because they want to.

The audience cannot be overlooked in this scene. Jesus speaks these words to His disciples, but he is aware that there are scribes present who are highly respected, even if by themselves. To use the word *child* is intentionally drawing a comparison to the uneducated and the brilliant, the ignorant and the knowledgeable.

He is making it clear that the gospel is received more willingly by the unwise and ignorant. It is for this reason Jesus thanks His Father that He has hidden the things of the gospel from the wise ones and revealed it so clearly to the ones who would be like *babes* (Matt. 11:25). God's grace is poured out, not because of your upstanding works and efforts. Jesus credits any good provision you have to the Father's pleasure to give it to you. The gift of grace has nothing to do with you or your abilities.

The scribes and Pharisees pestered Jesus as to why He associated with the lowly ones in society. He reminds them: "I have come to call sinners, not the self-righteous." Jesus did not focus His ministry on the ones who just could not get to church on time because of traffic, or the one who cannot seem to finish a full devotional book. His ministry was to the ones who were not only considered sinners, but also the exiles of the religious community. They certainly did not deserve this salvation, but it is these who open themselves more freely to the rescue Jesus offers. They knew they could not trust their own mechanisms to earn them anything, and it is that precise awareness that allows them to understand grace far better than the Pharisees of the time and the Pharisaical churchgoers of our own time.

No longer do we need to attach our works to our worth. Gone are the times when we have to marry our devotional life to our deservedness. We cannot desire God's attention, but deny his affection.[3] When we put an end to our tireless efforts to bargain with God, as if God owed us anything, we can rest in the love of the Father. We can know rescue from the dingy chamber of our own shame and vain efforts to earn what we have already been offered.

The question of nearly any presentation of God's grace is the same that Paul rhetorically poses in Romans 6: "So then should I continue to sin so that grace may increase?" What is the answer to anyone who does sin so their grace may increase? What about those who will say, "I have reason and excuse to sin. I can sin because PC said God does not care what I have done; God will love me"? I would point to the outstanding picture of grace that is my marriage.

I vowed to love Tonya and cherish her as a gift of God's grace. I would be naïve to say I will always do these things without tripping. There will be times I will not honor Tonya perfectly. There will be times I will not cherish her and hold her in the regard in which she should be held. There will be times she does not receive love from me as she needs, desires, and deserves.

Now, will she give up on me and divorce me? No! She will go on loving me though I have hurt her. But my hurting her is not the most serious transgression. The deepest cut the fact that, when I fail to love Tonya as I ought to, I have broken an eternal covenant we set in place through spoken vows. Each time I do not love, honor, and cherish her, I break a covenant. She still loves me. I do not deserve that.

Now imagine you were good friends with Tonya, and she came continuously to you about her bum of a husband. Suppose she told you how many times he had emotionally wrecked her with absolutely no regard. Suppose she told you how many times he unabashedly destroyed the promise he made to her. Suppose you knew these things. Would you be inclined to say, "Well, Tonya, that is great! Now your grace to him may increase."

I am compelled to realize how much grace Tonya really does show me, and how much of an idiot I would be if I paid no mind of her grace and continually abused it. Sure, she may always forgive me and love me, but in the end I would only be abusive. Instead, I see how much she forgives and loves me despite my broken promises, and I desire even more to love and serve her.

Such is God's grace! Do I just abuse it or does His grace drive me to a realization of my disregard? In the former case, when people abuse God's grace, Bonhoeffer said those people have a faulty understanding of grace, a type of grace he called "cheap grace." Brennan Manning called it "riding the coat tails of grace." However, when we truly accept the shocking gift of God's grace, it demands an affected response.

The story is told of a man bought in slave trade. Once the purchase had been finalized, his new master broke the shackles from his feet and hands, saying, "I bought you to set you free." After a pause packed with confusion and emotion, the man spoke with humility, "Because you have bought me to set me free, I will serve you for the rest of my life."

Grace does not give us a license to sin. In fact, the one who knows the gospel in the heart shuts down his toilsome machine of effort and serves his Rescuer in response. The heart of the one who knows this love is willing to serve Jesus the rest of his life because he was bought with a price in order to be set free.

Once I come face to face with the real gospel of Jesus, it will well up within me either a joyous appreciation or a rebellious resentment. This is highlighted very clearly between the child and the scribe. Many of us, particularly many Americans, resent a vital part of the gospel, namely its giftedness. Once we are face to face with the fact that we have to accept a gift rather than give and give and give of our devoted efforts, we become resentful of the gospel.

The gospel makes clear that we are "justified by his grace as a gift, through the redemption that is in Jesus Christ" (Rom. 3:24). "We cannot earn or win anything from God; we must either receive it as a gift or do without it," said Oswald Chambers.[4] This is a stark challenge to the way many of us try to understand the gospel. If you are not receiving it as a gift but are instead trying to work for it with all your own efforts, you are missing it. If you are trying to work and earn God's love, you are choosing to do without it.

The gospel is a gift and is to be received. It does not require your giving or your work. It is just as much selfish pride for me to refuse a gift, because in that refusal I make more of myself and less of God. This is the danger in not having a firm grasp of the true gospel—our works and efforts begin to be more intent on fabricating a beautiful picture of ourselves than on the gift and grace of God. We begin to attach our own self-worth to our ability to do enough right things. Too many Christians are trying to win God's love instead of accepting it with gratitude and humility.

The guest list for Jesus' meals featured the filthy and the unacceptable by the society's standards, but you cannot overlook the impact these meetings must have had on those broken people. They were accepted as peers in those moments. Nothing was held against them. This is one of the clearest expressions of the love of God incarnate in the person of Jesus Christ. He brings peace, hope, and dignity to those with whom He sits. In these moments, they are rescued from something deeper than we often acknowledge.

When Jesus shares a moment with someone who is regularly shoved to the gutter and berated by the world around him or her, he or she is freed from a prison of self-hatred. The very presence of Jesus with the destitute and the broken challenges them to no longer cloud their opinion of themselves with the truth of who they are. In the presence of Jesus, they no longer have to be afraid of the attacks on their identity from others or themselves. Can I trust in God's image of me instead of my tainted view?

Can you see how vital it is to be close to Jesus? Closeness to God is our ultimate good (Ps. 73:28). We all have within us a dingy chamber darkening the deep stone walls of our broken hearts, where a familiar voice screams for something more. We scream out for God to come closer, and the great truth of the Christmas story is that Jesus makes that closeness possible.

We do not pursue a generic god with a generic faith. We cannot be spiritual in a generic way. God came close as the skin and bone of your own forearm, and He said, "Call me Jesus. Call me Immanuel, God with us!" Sometimes I believe God showed up to shepherds because He goes to those who have time to listen. The possibility of this rescuing closeness is only closed off from those too busy to pay attention.

We are often moving and going so frantically that God's presence and blessing cannot land upon us. If God's peace descends like a dove, I am all but swatting it away with my hectic grasping after success. My priority is to be concentrated on Christ. His closeness— not my success—is my ultimate good. I spend too much of my heart, mind, energy, and time comparing myself against an impossible standard. Closeness to Jesus is our ultimate good. For it is in that closeness, where the Father's grace and love are heavier than the bags we shift from shoulder to shoulder, our bedraggled hearts are able to find rest and rescue.

The trouble with this closeness is that for many of us, as soon as we first came to Jesus, we quit coming to Jesus. Once we accepted Jesus as our Lord, we quit accepting Him as our Lord. Many of us began to follow Him but soon forgot His call to remain with Him (John 15:1-12). In those moments, we will certainly run dry. We drift away from the connection with Jesus and then wonder why our faith does not seem as refreshing as it was before.

Think of it like this: I could shave my face one day better than anyone has ever shaved a face in all of history. I would be enormously proud of my accomplishment, and such an act of sheer brilliance would warrant some honor. But I would still have to shave again the next day. One brilliant act of dedication does not negate the need for ongoing devotion to shaving. In the same way, one great moment of coming to Jesus must be followed by a lifetime of coming to Jesus.

Paul speaks to our tendency to wane from this connection to the closeness of Jesus when he employs us to "walk in [Jesus], rooted and built up in Him and established in faith" (Col. 2:6-7). Can you remember the first time you came to Jesus? Can you remember when all the obstacles you once knew seemed to be demolished in an instant, and you came running? Do you remember all the shame and guilt of your heart melting away in that moment? Remember when you knew you did not have the power or courage within yourself to surrender, but something made it entirely possible for you to submit yourself to the rescue provided in Christ? Remember when you trusted Jesus and came running, despite your unfaithfulness, your fears, your shame, or your guilt? Do you remember when you finally came to Jesus?

Think of that moment, feel that moment again, and then attach it to your attempt to remain in Him today. There are still temptations and struggles to keep you from the closeness that is your ultimate good. You will still shift toward a focus on your sin, and your heart will break under the weight of your guilt and shame. All of the goodness of being near to God will be available, and you will still try and fail at earning it. After all, you know yourself so well.

Romans 5:10 reminds us that if Jesus would rescue us when we were still staggering in our sin without hope, why would He not do so now that you are a child of God? This is a pretty important question you have to answer yourself. I do not mean you have the right answer (I know the right answer), but I mean you have to know the true answer with yourself at this point as you read this very page. By relentless trust you first came to Jesus, and it is by the same sort of trust that you remain in and walk with Jesus.

In more than a decade of full-time ministry with college students and young adults, I can point to a few very significant moments when the imprint of ministry was more heavily made on me. One of those moments unfolded during a teaching series on John 15. We had walked together through what it means to remain in Christ, and I wondered how much of our discussion had surpassed the mind to take the heart. On a Wednesday afternoon, one of my students posted a picture to a social media site of a beautiful sky and the tops of a tree line. The caption she posted read, "I am taking a break to entangle my heart with His." I thought to myself, "That's it! That is what I want to do."

Once I shared it with the group, it took off. Suddenly the hashtag #entanglement began to take over all of our social media outlets. Instead of sharing about our "quiet time" or "devotions," we would speak of our "entanglement time." We became a community obsessed with entangling our hearts with Jesus. God met us tenderly in return.

When something is tangled, any movement of one piece often gets it even more entangled with the whole, to the point that the mess becomes impossible to separate. I want to be so close to the heart of Jesus that I cannot be separated. The only way for that to happen is through an ongoing entanglement. This is what allows us to become men and women who truly know how to love Jesus with our heart below the machine. "Authentic disciples may have stumbled and frequently fallen, endured lapses and relapses, gotten handcuffed to the fleshpots and wandered into the far country," Brennan Manning wrote, "yet, they kept coming back to Jesus."[5] This is the mark of real followers of Jesus who have allowed His grace and love to take the heart.

THE WELL-OILED MACHINE

I CRAMMED FOUR years of college into five. As a ministry major I never attended church once through four of those five years. Like many others, as I studied the beginnings of the Church and Christ's intentions for it, I discovered a picture of how it ought to be, which was incongruent with my experience of the actual Church. I wasn't alone in this discovery, and like many college students, I decided, "Well! Then I am not going."

However, I gave little thought to this conflict between my lack of church attendance and the major I was pursuing. A friend listened to my reasons for not attending church. She was a patient listener who was open to what I had to say—until one day during my fifth year. She asked, "If you are so opinionated about how the Church ought to be, don't you think you are the one who most needs to be a part of the Church?" I knew she was right.

"I couldn't go to church; it's full of hypocrites." It is a common objection to Christianity. This statement says hypocrisy takes away the validity of Christianity, but there are two reasons this statement and the belief in what it says have to be debunked. First, it is true, and second, it does not make any sense.

To say Christians are hypocrites is true. In fact, most people are hypocrites. As long as an imperfect humanity tries to model after any ideal lifestyle and belief system, people will always be hypocrites. Ideal lifestyles of any sort take work, and we generally have to work through our imperfect realities to make them happen. This means mistakes will happen. It means not everyone is prepared to be perfect, but we still move forward. No church is full of hypocrites; there are almost always a few empty seats for you.

Secondly, it is frustrating to hear the objection to Christianity on the grounds of Christians being hypocrites because it does not make logical sense. In fact, this objection commits a logical fallacy of trivial objection—it focuses on the wrong thing. It focuses on insignificant things while ignoring the main point. The main point of being a Christian is whether or not a person believes Jesus Christ. Could it be possible Jesus was from Nazareth? Could it be possible God is a God of phenomenal love? Could it be possible the cross was real and accomplished what it says it does? Could all of these things be possible *even if* Christians are hypocrites?

Hypocritical Christians do not make Christianity false. Hypocrisy and sinful Christians do not disprove the cross. No matter how well people think of themselves, no person is truly without hypocrisy. Sinful Christians prove Christianity's gospel even more. They prove that imperfect people are still able to be Christians and followers of Jesus. Hypocrisy does not disprove God. It only proves that imperfect people are desperately in need of a savior. That is pretty good news to me.

You cannot love the groom and hate His bride, and I have come to dearly love the Church. I quit looking for the perfect church when every church I went to, I found myself in attendance. The challenge is for each of us to sort out the good from the bad in order to take hold of what is still sustainable. It means "naming and exorcising the curses—not cursing the people themselves, who may have left you stranded with a boogeyman God."[6] I tried rejecting all the things I could not personally fix about the Church, and my own rejection made no sense.

The established church has become a force in many of our lives. It has become a well-oiled machine with conferences, books, and viral videos making up tiny pieces that build that machine. "Numbers impress us... We measure churches by how many members they boast. We are wowed by big crowds."[7] We are obsessed with maintaining these great machines built with big budgets and bigger buildings.

Big churches are not the trouble. In fact, large churches are accomplishing great things that smaller churches may not be able to facilitate. The trouble is that a well-oiled machine of a church is made up of Christians who have made machinery out of their faith. Grace does not work in the confines of a machine faith. We want grace and miracles, but we go on operating in ways to make miracles unnecessary. We pump out all the right answers about our need for grace, and not works—but everything about the way we walk through life contradicts our claims.

Our culture has a difficult time understanding grace. Instead of grace, we live by these mottos:

"You earn what you get."

"You made your bed. Now lie in it."

"You only get what you deserve."

"What doesn't kill me only makes me stronger."

They may be beneficial to the businessmen in Silicon Valley, but they do not belong in the gospel of grace. The gospel ceases to be the gospel when it comes to look more and more like the American Dream. The gospel is not a do-it-yourself project you maintain, and yet so many Christians attempt to make a DIY machine out of faith.

Another sign of the machine replacing the heart in Christian living is our attempt to get ahead of God. The grand operation of salvation absolutely must begin with the initiative God makes toward us, but too often our faith begins with the self. However, the gospel makes clear that we are the responders. It is not about the virtue and clout we can acquire because of our efforts, but about our response to the gift God gives to each one of us. We are exceptionally unable to fix our own limitations, get rid of our troubles, or reach the pie in the sky of Christian maturity on our own. Still we hammer away at our faith machine and miss the heart of the gospel.

What you read in these pages, encouragements for Christians to believe and live the gospel, does not always reflect perfectly my life's actions. I struggle as you likely do in living out the way we wish we could. Thus the fight to do what we want to do instead of doing what we do not want to do, and the tendency to do what we do not want to do. Although I am writing to encourage my fellow travelers to embrace the gospel, I am also a daily-broken human being with imperfect feelings, hurts, pains, angers, and frustrations. I write about God's love and grace better than I practice it in my life. The concepts I write about, valid as they may be, are still hard to live. Does this mean I do not want to live them? Of course not!

I sometimes find myself shaking a fist and yelling, "Practice what you preach!" But I know my haranguing of pastors, teachers, Christians, and churches is not always warranted. Who am I to say they are *not* trying to practice what they preach? Who am I to presume that they are not, like me, simply children of an Abba who understands they are humans who cannot wish themselves into perfection and righteousness? They struggle to do what they wish they would, but it does not and should not take away from their exhausting desire to fight for righteousness, holiness, and unconditional love.

Our constant fight to build and repair ourselves, our fumbling about trying to earn God's love while hiding our narrow-mindedness and floundering in our pity parties, are a dizzying waste of time and a rejection of the heart of the gospel. There is a great difference between *making* a failure and *being* a failure, and only the former is true of a child of God. One only becomes a failure when they staple it onto their own identity. Our approach to the life of following Jesus is just as ridiculous as my believing that I could fix the actual machines in my home.

One has to search his mind and heart with unrelenting honesty to determine whether he really knows what grace is and is living according to a true understanding of grace. We use the term a tremendous amount, and as with anything that is overused, it can lose its power.

Grace is only given to the humble, not the proud. Grace is only given to the sinful who recognize their need. It is only given to the ones who acknowledge and confess their sinfulness and open themselves to grace. Only the ones who truly hunger and thirst for righteousness will be fully satisfied. Grace only makes sense to the ones prepared to be beggars at its door. "Beggars come with open hands to God, expecting Him to give us grace."[8] It does not appear to be given in as much measure to the ones who are wondering what is wrong with other sinners.

We have learned to recite the great theological phrase "justification by grace through faith" in much the same way we have learned to say "I asked Jesus into my heart," "I accepted Jesus into my life," and "I gave my life to Jesus." We have evolved mundane phrases for something Chesterton called a "furious love." This is a grace and love that does what no other god or person has ever done; this furious love loves broken sinners. All the gods humans have created cannot stand sinners, and here is our God who gives an immense mercy that restores a relationship with this mess of people.

Jesus had gained an enormous following after He taught and healed several people. Just yesterday we were walking, and He was brought to a man who had been paralyzed his whole life. You know, you never get used to the things Jesus does!

I was certain Jesus would heal this guy, but the first thing He did was forgive all the sins of this paralyzed man. Let me tell you; the church people were so angry. I mean, I am a church person, but I was not so frustrated as much as I was intrigued by the whole thing. It was then that Jesus told a paralyzed man to just get up and walk.

And he did!

We were all pretty amazed. You sort of have to be amazed when you witness firsthand the work of Jesus.

As we kept walking and following Jesus, there was an awestruck murmur in the crowd. What giant miracle would He do next? Well, I will tell you. It may not seem like a miracle to you, but allow me to assure you it was!

Jesus saw this man, Matthew, which is important to know because none of us saw Matthew. We did our best to avoid and ignore him. You know when you walk through the mall and try to avoid the person selling a product from the kiosk? This is how we did not *see* Matthew.

But Jesus saw him. He approached Matthew and said, "Follow me!"

I laughed, quietly enough for only those around me to hear and raise their eyebrows in surprise.

We were believers, and if I might say so, we are pretty great people. This Matthew? He was not! He was a swindler, and we all knew it. We wondered if Jesus actually knew the type of person He just told to follow Him.

But this is not the miracle!

We and Matthew followed Jesus to Matthew's house. We crowded outside trying to see and hear what Jesus was up to in there, but if I am honest with you, I wanted to make sure Matthew did not manipulate Jesus like he had done to everyone else. It is funny how often I thought Jesus needed my help because He was clearly naïve to who those people really are. He needed me to keep Him and His reputation safe, you know?

It was not long before Matthew's whole crew of degenerates arrived. They were all eating and drinking with Jesus. They were listening to Him, and He listened to them. It seemed as though everyone's reputation changed around that table.

You might have missed the miracle! I certainly did.

Every encounter with Jesus affects your and His reputation. In one momentary encounter, Jesus went from the "great teacher and healer" to "a man who spends time with the dregs of society we like to avoid and ignore" (it is a long made-up name, I know!). Matthew and his crew went from "disgusting degenerates and manipulators" to "friends of Jesus."

Jesus heard our bickering and not-so-hushed criticism, and He reminded us He desires compassion, not sacrifice.

Following Jesus now involved my own reputation. If I was unwilling to invite outsiders into my life, I was unwilling to follow Jesus. After the fun of being an insider subsided, I had to decide whether I really wanted to risk my reputation to be a follower of Jesus.

Here is an epiphany that will change your life when you accept it: Jesus is only going to be a great rescue for those who realize they need Him. He comes to rescue those who are marginalized. He comes to give peace and restoration to the ones who have failed over and over again. He comes to the criminals, homeless, addicts, debt collectors, degenerate artists, and murderers of bodies and minds. He does not just talk to them. He sits with them. He is aware how His dinner company affects His reputation among the straightedge religious officials.

You cannot overlook this choice Jesus makes over and over in Scripture, because the gospel really is this good. The salvation, peace, and blessing of Jesus Christ belong to the filthy and wrecked, not to the ones who keep a safe distance. Jesus forgave the excuse-ridden paralytic and the despised tax collector.

The gospel is not a pretty suburb for the self-righteous. The Kingdom Jesus speaks of is not a country club with manicured regulations about who is allowed to be there. The Kingdom belongs to people not trying to be cleaner than they are, because the gospel only lands on those who know they need it. It is for a much grander, more unattractive, and more insecure cast of people who have actually known the seasick up-and-down moral wrestling. The gospel will only make sense to the ones who know and act like they need it.

These are the ones Jesus sat with until their reputations were changed. These are the ones who Jesus still comes to sit with today. The Light is only known in its fullest by those who have stared into the real darkness of their own failure, past, or cracked choices. The Church should not look so much like an art gallery of perfect specimens as a triage unit for the real sinners in need of grace and rescue. This is the place I need.

Can you find the Good News in a place full of the damaged in need of mercy and rescue? The Good News is found in that I can stop lying to myself about who I am below the Christian cosmetics. When the Church looks more like Jesus' dinner guests, I know I am welcomed even though the battle with my anger, shame, and lust may stir in me. When I really understand the gospel, I know God loves me and welcomes me as I am.

When we are honest with ourselves, we have to admit we are big boxes of contradictions. We have built a beautiful machine and put a "Faith" sticker on the outside. Our beautiful machine keeps breaking down, as it inevitably must. Each time it breaks down, we are surprised. We did everything right! How could this happen? It is in the pile of our broken-down machinery parts that we can see the heart of the gospel that still beats slowly for each of us. It is here we are able to admit we have some shadows.

We build this machine not only in efforts to cover and miss the heart, but also to encase and cover our own shadows. Our machine proves how little we really believe God's love for us. It proves how little we believe the things we say about the gospel. We build machines to produce pretty products. We are churning out nice-looking people with fancy gadgets of faith and hiding away the true beating heart that tries to love and relate to God through all the broken places. It is a question of trust.

Faith is trust. Most people today equate faith with belief; they define faith as a belief in God. When you look at Scripture, many did not need faith to believe in God. They knew God existed. They saw Him do incredible things that no one could deny. Faith had more to do with whether or not you really trusted God. There is an enormous difference here, and we have to use the terms properly if we are to look beneath our broken machines.

Our broken machines always present us with a decision: Do you really trust God loves you? Can you accept that you are accepted by God even though your pretty machine is terribly broken? The gospel screams out to you: you are not just a bitter shrew, a man obsessed with getting rich, a woman stuck walking through life without passion or desire, a young person who wants the thrill of being an adult without the responsibility. You may be uncertain, incompetent, misunderstood, or haunted by your past. Anxiety, depression, and self-doubt may ride you hard nearly every day. But you are not *only* these things! You are accepted and loved and liked by God. Do not project your perception of yourself onto Abba's perception of you.

No matter where your machine has brought you, there is no need to cower before Jesus. We are so obsessed with our strengths that we learned with great tools and assessment tools. Then we study them and build on them. We form them and make them requirements for ministry. But Jesus says, "My grace is sufficient for you, for my power is made perfect in weakness," so "boast all the more gladly in your weaknesses, so that the power of Christ may rest upon you" (2 Cor. 12:9). Again, our strengths are important for good leadership and work, and God does wire us with each of them, but the gospel does not depend on your strengths.

When the church rejects people who are fully accepted by Jesus—when we demonize and demean homosexuals, shame addicts, vilify other races—the machine takes the heart. Jesus sat with the corrupt and changed their reputation. The truly ungodly actions are the ones laid out by the machines designed to keep out the ones Jesus welcomed. "Any church that will not accept that it consists of sinful men and women, and exists for them, implicitly rejects the gospel of grace."[9]

I once heard a speaker read through Romans 8, specifically the passage asking us, "What can separate us from the love of God...nothing can separate us from the love of God." He went on to speak for maybe two minutes and posed the question: "Now dialogue with me for a couple minutes. What things separate you from the love of God?"

Hands shot up all over the room! Everyone had an answer.

"Sin!"
"Temptations!"
"Peers!"
"Bad choices!"
"Shame and guilt!"
"Expectations!"

I was thunderstruck! We *just* read the passage two minutes before. Had we already forgotten? Did we really understand the first time? I could not believe it. We had just stood up and read aloud as a community in one voice that said, "*Nothing* can separate us from the love of God." Why is this so hard for us to trust that we forgot a pointblank reading of it just two minutes later?

Something is terribly wrong here!

We are convinced that so many things can actually separate us from the love of God. Yet, in a rare instance, the Bible is wonderfully black and white on this issue.

I am of the mind and heart that we can be separated from God, but we cannot be separated from His love.

Living in California has separated me from my family, with most of America between us. I am not as close to my mom, dad, brothers, nieces, or nephews as I used to be. We have been separated by geography, a choice I made nearly 15 years ago. We have been separated by growth and life decisions. Does my mom love me less than she ever did? No! Has my dad removed his love from me? Of course not! Have my brothers disowned me? No! They all still love me, and I still love all of them even though we are separated. Nothing can separate me from the love of my family.

Yes! Our sin separates us from God. Our choices will sometimes place a divide between God and us. When I spend less time with God, it results in lost intimacy and connection. I can become disconnected and even separated from God.

But...

Nothing, absolutely nothing, can separate me from the love of God!

I wonder why that is so hard for us to understand. It took me years to realize the difference and now it seems clear as the sky. It is so simple.

It is painful enough to know we have convinced ourselves that God does not love us when we sin or blow it, but there is something even more painful to my heart—when our inability to understand the gospel spills over into the world around us. Out of our conviction that our actions and decisions can separate us from God's love, we have enforced this ridiculousness on other dirty saints and sinners around us. We have convinced them also that God does not love them because of their sin and life decisions. Something is heartbreakingly wrong here!

When I used to work in the department of student life at a small liberal arts university, one of my students did graphic design for some extra cash. One of his bosses was a gay nightclub owner and author. He had been putting finishing touches on a book and asked my student to read the manuscript. My student told me a lot of things he read in the book. The book is quite autobiographical and reveals a lot of this man's ideas of God. His main belief is God hates him. He does not say that Christians hate him; he is convinced that *God* hates him. God has completely removed His love from this man as far as he is concerned.

Where did he get this perception?

He likely got it from the people who bear God's message and image. He likely got it from God's people who themselves seem to be convinced that people can be separated from God's love, and if they believe *they* can be separated from the love of God, then surely so would the homosexual nightclub owner. Some make signs of this message and scream it from a megaphone on the rooftops!

But let us be frank. We do not need signs or bullhorns on a street corner that remind us of this faulty belief, do we? We are capable enough in our minds and comments to condemn homosexuals, drunks, prostitutes, and Democrats to separation from God's love.

Why do we do this to people?

It appears we do it to ourselves as well. We have convinced ourselves that we can be and often are separated from the love of God. It is crazy enough that we have convinced ourselves of this, but something dies in the heart when we have convinced others of the same thing.

After more than a decade in full-time pastoral ministry, I am convinced that every Sunday, limping through the doors of our churches comes the gospel in bandages—sinners who cannot get rid of the fractured machine parts they have gathered throughout the week. Still, their showing up at all is a faint cry of desire to be close to God. After all, that desire is in each one of us, because the heart knows closeness to God is our ultimate good.

It is not only the visibly broken we have to focus on. It is vital that you recognize the potential for your manufactured machine of faith to be battered and shattered at any moment. You must not pretend your spiritual cosmetics are immune to the effects of loneliness, failure, discouragement, doubt, guilt, and shame. We cannot read these words and turn our eyes to the visibly sinful piles of people in our midst, because in turning our eyes to them we turn our eyes away from Jesus. We are sinking!

I am convinced that on the final day, as revealed in Revelation 7:9, there will only be the people who have shed the machine parts they spent a lifetime building and rebuilding. There will be only the ones who wanted to be faithful and devoted, who at times were wrecked, defeated, and worn down by the trials of life. They will come wearing only the ragged cloth of misfortune, but they will be those who at some point said, "This machine is broken. I will hold on to the heart that lies beneath."

THE LIP OF THE GRAND CANYON

HAVE YOU EVER sat on the shore of the ocean and looked out on the endless horizon and felt...small? Have you ever looked out the window of a plane to see quilted ground with its various patches, shapes, colors and felt like you are only a small part of a much larger whole? Have you ever thought about the countless people who have lived before you and the exponential more who will live after you and never have any idea who you are?

Have you ever gone up away from the light pollution of the city and sat under the bowl of stars? Have you ever looked at pictures in a textbook that look beyond the atmosphere we see into an expansive universe that our great grandparents never would have imagined? Have you ever gone out on a beautiful day or night and looked into the sky with astonishment? Have you ever seen an original Picasso? Have you ever seen something that just moved you?

All who have had these experiences can say they have *seen* such sights. But some have only seen it with their eyes, while others have seen it with their heart and soul. Some have only given a glance, and others have made sacred spaces out of those moments. This is beginning to get at what it means to engage our heart and soul beneath the machine.

Some people have a way of living deeper and fuller. Their circumstances may be the same as everyone else's. They breathe the same air, but they have an ability to see more, experience more, and enjoy more.

The presence of incredible things and amazing beauty makes you feel sad for people who are in such a hurry that they never fully appreciate what is in front of them. I wonder if God feels the same sadness. Think of the creation account in Genesis 1. The Artist reveals his dramatic masterpiece, and His reaction is the refrain at the end of each creation day. God saw all that He had made, and said, what? "It is good!" After He created human beings, He said, "It is *very* good!" God is in awe of his own creation. Read that again and think about it! He is in wonderment of His work.

What do we do when God seems distant and hard to see? There are those times when God seems so difficult to know. In those moments, I find encouragement in Romans 1:20. "For His invisible attributes, namely, his eternal power and divine nature, have been clearly perceived, ever since the creation of the world, in the things that have been made." We are able to see God in the things He has made. If we took more time to notice these things, we would come to see Him and know Him more clearly.

Think for a moment about the Grand Canyon as one example. Imagine standing on the very lip of the Grand Canyon, and you are one of those who can truly soak in the absurd beauty. If you stood there, tiny by comparison, you realize how great this incredible work truly is. As you look out on the majesty of the Grand

Canyon, reflect on how something as grandiose is only a tiny part of God's creation. If this stunning erosion from the Colorado River is only a faint glimpse of God's full glory, you have to wonder, "What must *He* be like?"

Would you stand at the lip of the Grand Canyon unaffected? Perhaps some would. A huge problem of our day is that we have lost all sense of wonder. Nothing amazes us anymore. We grow more and more numb to the marvelous! We forget how powerful God really is because none of these things startle us. Remember when the Grand Canyon was amazing before seeing it in a million pictures? We lose the sense of wonder when giant trees, natural running streams, crashing waves, and enormous mountains are no longer a big deal. We see them every day. We forget the amazing things we learned in elementary school about how trees grow and how waves form. We forget all those things because we have learned about them and are no longer shocked.

Some of my dearest friends live in Malibu on the campus of Pepperdine University. The campus is built into the mountain looking out to the Pacific Ocean over the Pacific Coast Highway. The sliding glass door of my friends' house also affords them this beautiful view. During one of our visits to their home, Tonya said, "I could never get used to this view! It's so beautiful." Our friend responded, "Oh yeah! I forget that it's there."

What!?!

We do ourselves a great disservice. We do God a disservice when these things no longer amaze us. Praise is our astonishment expressed! We have come to overuse words like "awesome," and the result is a complete neutering of such words, not only in our vocabulary, but also in our experience of such things. In her clever

TED talk, Jill Shargaa pleads, "Please, please people. Let's put the 'awe' back in 'awesome.'"[10]

David in the Old Testament had a habit of doing this and then writing what his mind and heart could muster from the experience. He did not even have our technology to see distant galaxies and worlds. He only looked at the sky we all see, and he felt astonishingly small.

Grab a Bible or open a Bible app right now, and turn to Psalm 8. Begin to picture David taking a leisurely stroll outside at night. He might have his fingers interlocked behind his head. Picture him staring into the sky; he could only think of God. He let out a deep sigh of amazement and penned Psalm 8.

This psalm is a hymn celebrating and honoring God. David is taken by the astonishment of God. In this moment of awe he feels...small. He is struck with the realization that he does not know very much. When was the last time you were struck with the realization of just how small you are?

David begins to wonder and wrestle with the character and identity of God. This experience thrusts David into a relational encounter. Don't miss it! In a moment of being utterly small and insignificant, he also meets this expansive God in an emotional experience. He cries out for someone he cannot see, and he is met in a very real encounter. It is an eruption of relationship.

He starts off addressing God: "O LORD, our LORD!" The Hebrew word used here for "LORD" is *Jehovah*, which is to say "our prop, our support, our mainstay." David exclaims, "How majestic is your name," which is to say,

"I have no words. My words fall very flat when I try to describe or grasp you."

A sense of awe and amazement is often all you need to meet God in a real way. How often will children tell us of a God whom we have forgotten? Children have a phenomenally real encounter with God, and it is not due to naivety. It is because they have a sense of trust and awe that we lost years ago. God has a bizarre kingdom containing only the humble who realize how small they are, who are content to realize how small they are. David knows this in verse 2 when he writes, "From the lips of children and infants you have ordained praise."

Wonder and awe are primitive human emotions. They are so primal that they are the Creator's reaction to His own creation. I will never forget the moment I first saw my daughters and held each of them in my hands. I will never forget the rolling waves of the open ocean off the coast of Mexico. I will never forget the scene under the stars in Avon, Colorado, away from the light pollution of the city. Have you ever had an epiphany like this, a moment when heaven seemed to overrun earth, a moment when it seemed the presence of God was so tangible? Thank God, because in those moments you are discovering something deeper and greater than just what you see. In moments like those, you are getting a glimpse of what it means to love God with all of your soul. It is a natural reaction. In that moment, you are doing exactly what God was doing in the beginning. We are doing more than just reacting—we are loving God.

Most of us have lost large parts of our heart and soul. When we lose our sense of awe and wonder, we really lose a piece of our heart: the capacity for love. The machine is being built around the heart. Could it be possible we have given God a passing glance instead of really knowing what it means to recognize how holy He is? Could it be possible we have settled for a god that fits into the constraints of our imaginations, instead of the God in Ephesians 3:20, who is able to do immeasurably more than we can think or imagine?

Augustine said, "*Si comprehende, non est Deus*"—if you can understand it, it is not God. Most commonly God has to break in or break down our machinery in order to get through to our heart. There must come a point when God breaks through our attempts at controlling everything around us. There has to be a point where we are willing to experience what "no eye has seen, no ear has heard, no mind has conceived...what God has prepared for those who truly love Him" (1 Cor. 2:9).

I can remember as a child being afraid of things called thunderstorms. These Californians I have lived with for many years keep saying, "PC, we *know* what thunderstorms are," and I keep telling them after more than 13 years since moving here from Indiana, "No, you do not!" I am speaking of thunderstorms that literally shake the walls and floors of your home. Rain pours down with extraordinary force and from all directions.

As a child, you are terrified of these things. You *know* the thunder is going to kill you if you stay in your bed, and the only place thunder will consider off limits is your parents' bed. So you risk your life for the few seconds it takes to run to your mom and dad's bed like you are a soldier in an action movie, miraculously faster than the spray of helicopter machine guns.

You know who Nikola Tesla is, right? He is one of history's most remarkable inventors. He is recorded to have had a ritual during thunderstorms. He would sit on a couch near the window, and every time lightning struck or the thunder clapped, he would rise to his feet and applaud God. This is a tradition I taught my daughters a couple of years ago. Whenever they experience a California "thunderstorm," they run to the window and clap. It does my heart a lot of good. Now, you can get "thunderstorm" in ambient noisemakers meant to sooth you to sleep. I love thunderstorms. I no longer fear for my life, because I have lost the awe of tremendous thunderstorms.

David would frequently look into the sky with wonder and awe, but he would always do so in amazement of his God. He is so astonished that he is unable to grasp it all at once. He is so overwhelmed with the presence of God in this moment that he can only ask a very important question in verse 4:

"What is man that you are mindful of him?"

He has a deeper sense of wonder at the power of God, and yet the intimacy of God's concern for us leaves him in even more admiration. When he realizes how huge and extensive God is, David realizes at the same time how small and insignificant he is by comparison. This is more than just growing our soul. This is worship.

Worship in its most primitive definition is wonder. It is standing in awe of the Creator. How often are you in awe of God on a Sunday morning? How often do you allow yourself to be more concerned with sitting in wonder of God than you are with the things of programming and technical arrays?

When a baby is born, it takes months for their visual resolution to develop. They have to acquire depth perception and visual range. Our eye for wonder develops much the same way. The Holy Spirit gives us depth perception; He opens our eyes to see the ordinary miracles that surround us.

The world is saturated with the Holy. It is full of God's presence. It is the very water we swim in each day. When we realize the truth of Ephesians 4:6 that God is over all, through all, and in all, there arises a saddening reality on our part. We realize God is present everywhere, and we still miss Him entirely in the course of a day and week.

We need what the great spiritual formation writer, Richard Foster, calls the "prayer of examen of consciousness." We need to recognize what Erwin McManus calls divine moments in need of seizing. We need to practice with Brother Lawrence the presence of God.

Each day is full of God's presence, and my mind and heart need to be attentive to His presence. I need to prayerfully reflect on the thoughts, feelings, and actions of my days to see how God has been at work around me and how I respond to those moments. Each day is my opportunity to be present where I am. God invites me to see and hear and respond to what is around me, and through it all, to discern the footprints of God.

What may God be doing in and through my kids today? What may God be inviting me into through the neighbor, the barista, the homeless man I come across today? What may God be teaching me or forming in me through the loss of a job, the loss of a loved one, a confusing circumstance, or a conflict in a relationship?

These are all divine moments when heaven invades earth. I need to have the same sort of awe and wonder that made my daughter see a beautiful sunset and rainbow and say, "Daddy, did you see what God painted just for me?" More specifically, these are all moments heaven invades *my* world today. I only pray and ask that I have eyes to see and ears to hear.

What we see largely depends upon what we have experienced or not experienced. We see what we are looking for. We do not see what we are not looking for. Therefore, wonder, or lack thereof, simply reveals what is in our heart. Loving God with all of our heart begins with wonder, a soul flooded with the glory of God, a heart awed by beauty and mystery.

David is not only amazed by how small he is; he is even further amazed God would have an intentional relationship with him. "What is man that you are mindful of him, the son of man that you care for him?"

Many of us have no problem accepting and reflecting on how great God is. We like God to be so big that we do not have to try to come close to Him. We like to think of how enormous God is, but we get pretty cowardly when it comes to accepting God's love for us. When was the last time you intentionally sat in awe of God's love for you? Too many of us cannot imagine being loved by anyone, much less the God of perfection and glory. It is for exactly this reason I asked when you last allowed yourself to be in awe of this fundamental truth. God loves you! God himself is certainly too great for me to understand and fully articulate, but the fact He loves me is the most astounding reality of it all. Do you know yourself as loved? Can you, even for a moment, stand in awe of that fact?

Having traveled the country for nearly two decades as a speaker and evangelist, I am dazed by the outright denial of God's massive love. This same enormous God is described as Love in the Bible, and it is the Love that makes so many Christians fidget in their seats. The cynics may be the well-groomed professionals who like to speak about the sovereignty of God, because it is a word they recognize, to the shacked-up Christian who only knows the God of punishment who insists on a perfect standard.

Our resistance to this love can be traced back to a number of things, and a wound is likely in the soil. It may be wounds inflicted by the church, by our parents, or by circumstances we have crawled through on bloodied knees and palms. Regardless of where the defiance comes from, we have to look with awe and wonder upon the truth of God's love for us.

Instead of rejecting the truth of God characterized as Love, when grace takes the heart beneath the machine, we have to reject the god who hovers over our head in search of our failure—the God who is unable to watch us fumble and ease an empathetic grin onto His face, the God who wants nothing to do with our day-to-day, the God who says, "You made your bed, now lie in it."

It is also necessary to reject the buddy Jesus who promises you Chicago pizza and rainbows every day. The heart beneath the machine realizes the gospel is still to be lived out right now on this dusty ground, but the heart still beats to the reality of God's Son coming close to us. The god of so many people I have known is way too trivial for me.

Here before you is the God who does not expect your perfect control of yourself before He will love you. It is truly awesome. For the ones whose machines have broken around them, this is the place where you can see that your breakage has not driven God away from you. The heart still beats, and He still meets you in that place.

Will we ever really understand the gospel of grace and God's love? *Could* we ever? It is a scandalous love affair we are enrapt in, you know? "We should be astonished at the goodness of God, stunned that He should bother to call us by name, our mouths wide open at His love, bewildered that at this very moment we are standing on holy ground."[11] Every moment Jesus taught in parables, His antagonists were red-faced in embarrassment.

But trust in the gospel of grace cultivates confident followers of Jesus. A loving God nurtures loving people. Can you see how great the love of God is? His compassion gushes out to every man and woman. Trust in the heart of the gospel looks like awe and wonder that leads to the acceptance of and turning to God for the gift He has already offered to you.

On the other hand, once the machine takes the heart, we come to be oblivious to the love affair in front of our faces. The Lover of our soul pursues us and moves to us, and we play so hard to get. Our prayers dry up and crumble. There has to be a willingness to be loved recklessly. "Take this kind of willingness into the prayers you pray in the stillness and silence of your heart, and you will be seduced by God, just like Abraham was."[12] With mechanical faith, our prayer and efforts come to be entirely oblivious to the outright seduction of true love.

David's phrase in Psalm 8, "that you care for him," means "to attend to." It implies more than just God's concern *for* you; it implies God's action and emotion *toward* you. Some earlier translations of this verse say, "What is man that you should visit him," and I like that quite a bit more. God is inviting us to see faith as a journey toward and with Him.

David's question is not a self-centered one. It is about

the relationship. It requires a sense of trust and awe many of us have seen die away as we have grown older. We have to remember what it was like to have the trust and wonder of a child. We have to learn how to embrace wonder and really lean into the mystery of our faith in God. The mystery of how great God is, yes, but also the great mystery that this great God would know you and love you. Not that He loves all people, or that he loves Billy Graham, Mother Teresa, or Rick Warren, but that He loves *you*! This sense of mystery, if you can remember it and be okay with it, will lead you into a deeper, more intimate relationship with God than you will ever know.

One pastor tells the story of his daughter bursting into his home office and saying, "Daddy! Did you know if you are quiet enough, you can hear God telling you He loves you?" Distracted, the dad asks her to repeat herself. She says, "Daddy! Did you know if you are quiet enough, you can hear God telling you He loves you?"

She paused for a few seconds, looked up with surprise, and said, "See! I told you!"

Christianity is not an ethic. It is not a philosophy of life. It is a love affair. It is the thrill of loving and being loved by Jesus Christ, who sits present with you now, and He brings you closer to God so you can become more than just a good person. He invades our machinery so we can become prophets and lovers with a touch of wonder and awe who recognize a world that explodes with the Creator's beauty.

Did you know if you stop, sit in wonder, and if you are quiet enough, you can hear God telling you He loves you?

YOUR GOD IS TOO SMALL [ANOTHER POEM]

If your god is relegated to conscience
that little voice in your head trained to speak
at the wave of your experience
your god is too small for me

If your god is only a projection of the distant father in your living room
who abused or neglected you
when a father was more important
than food or shelter
your god is too small for me

If your god failed you by not doing what you thought he ought
If your god is designed for your convenience and comfort
If your god is a white-haired old man who is more old-fashioned than old-aged
If your god is historically respected
but defective in your current complexity
your god is too small for me

If your god is less meek and more mild
piled with placid temperament
un-inspired
un-moved
un-intentional
If your god's emotional capacity for compassion is less than yours
your god is too small for me

If your god calls you to comfort
safe for the whole family
always "come unto me" but never "go out in my name"
If your god has never flushed your face or stolen your words
with waves of open ocean or mountains
that mouse your vocabulary
If your god does not leave you in awe of amazing grace
so unbalanced
you clamor to conceive it
your god is too small for me

If your god abides by your contracts and cold contingencies
If your god only works through the cogs of machinery
you have manufactured
for a factory of formulas to faith

If your god is white
middle-class
Republican

If your God created you in His image and you returned the favor
your god is too small for me

Because my God
is not contained in bullet points pressed on a page
by those arrogant enough to think they could grasp Him

If you are searching for a god small enough to see
tiny enough to taste or touch with trust displaced

If your soul is not sandbagged or beautifully nagged
by a God who won't. Stop. Calling. Your. Name.

If you do not praise your God for poetry, music, and art
a baby's smile or a full coffee cart
for brazen horizons and seas
a resounding storm or a tender breeze
If your god does not leave you in love with beauty
that makes your soul scream
"THIS is what life should be!"

If you are searching for a god you can wrangle like a mustang
with a rope made of frayed twine and managed reason
If you need a being who will obey your beckoning to submit
to your five senses and incomprehensive pretenses

then this poem might not be for you
and my God might be
too big for you

WALKING THE GANGLY WIRE

"LET YE WITHOUT sin keep your boring self away from me." Once I posted this to my wall, a friend teased in return: "Sin is fun, huh?" I could only reply, "Of course! But perfect people are *not*!"

Christians appear to be blindsided by the fact that it is even possible for Christian couples to get to a point where divorce happens. We cannot understand how a Christian could relapse into addiction and moral failure. How could a Christian keep falling prey to the weight of unhealthy relationships?

Christians forget they hold themselves to a different standard, but that far from makes them morally superior. There is a common perception among Christians, false though it may be, that becoming a Christian brings them innate morality exceeding that of non-Christians. It is for this reason a common frustration non-Christians have with Christians is "they think they are better than everyone else." We absolutely do!

No matter how many *Not Perfect; Just forgiven* stickers you put on your car, we cannot dispute the fact we have come to be convinced of our innate moral superiority to those who do not follow Christ—although we know the fact is that we are a new creation, *not* a perfect creation.

We are still a new creation living in the same humanity prone to temptation, sin, and failure.

I strive so hard to live with the most excellent virtue, in absolute piety, in "Christian perfection" of sorts that I become more strained, confined, and closed in. We can be so narrowly focused upon upholding the rules and expectations we place on ourselves that we forget the relationship we were intended to have. I think of the comparison between the prodigal and his brother. I think of the difference in levels of intimacy with the father. In brokenness and humility, the prodigal experiences far greater intimacy with the father than does his sinless, pious, self-righteous brother.

The true picture of Christian disciples is one of men and women who are able to praise God for all things, including the need of rescue that their own sin produces. It is he who is not obsessed with the perfect presentation of himself and his spirituality. It is she who is not complacent with and shackled by the practical life. It is he who strives more for the relationship than the rules and understands he has failed and will fail again, but recognizes that God expects more failure from him than he ever does of himself. It is she who realizes she does not have to come groveling to God with a clear and complete list of her sins and failures in order to be forgiven.

The prodigal's father did not ask for an explanation, and Jesus did not ask the adulterous woman for an apology or confession. The true Christian disciples realize they will not be judged now or in the end for their sins because they have already been judged and found not guilty, but they know God desires that they show up in His embrace and accept His love.

As a child I was always asked the same question

every year as Christmas approached, which was likely posed to you when you were growing up: "Have you been a good little boy or girl?" What a question! This is the closest I would have known to my own Day of Atonement as reflected in the Old Testament. For an entire year? We only ask this question each Christmas, so we must be talking about the time between now and last Christmas. Do you know how hard it is for me to be a good little boy for an entire year? Just mark it down as an impossibility. But I always got Christmas presents regardless of my flawed year-in-review.

The Jewish people had a certain thought concerning the Messiah's coming: they would have to collectively honor the Sabbath fully for four straight weeks in order to usher in the coming of the Messiah. Like broken human beings, it often would not last a day. They were convinced that they had to earn and deserve the coming of a Messiah to deliver them. But Jesus does not wait until you deserve Him, because you will never deserve Him. You will never deserve the freedom and forgiveness He offers as a gift.

Jesus is not a reward for the righteous or a prize for the pious. Jesus was and is a gift for the imperfect. He is good news for the faulty ones who try hard but are unable to live out the perfection they wish they could manage.

I will never be good enough to earn His gift, but that is the good news of the gospel. That is the heart beneath the machine. It is a gift for the broken and sinful, not a prize for the perfect. The gospel is a paradox for our normal gift-giving practices. In the gospel beneath the machinery, the good little boy or girl gets no gifts.

God speaks to Abraham and says, "I am God

Almighty; walk before me, and be blameless" (Gen. 17:1). Consistently throughout Scripture, there is reference to people being blameless before God. Blameless, not faultless! We know our list of faults cannot be denied, but God choses to find us blameless. This is humbling on the one hand and encouraging on another. It is humbling to know you are still not without fault. It is humbling to remember you still live on earth, short of perfection. It is good to have this humble reminder once you have been called *blameless*.

It is encouraging to know that though your life is bent toward destructive choices and faults, you can still be seen as blameless if you will be entangled with Jesus. May we learn to live blameless though not always faultless! There is pleasure in our Father's eyes in His declaration of our blamelessness.

We have so many things whirling in our hearts and minds regarding who we are and how we ought to perceive ourselves. The only one that matters is what God says to me and of me. What matters is how God feels toward me. After Jesus is baptized, His Father speaks of how He feels toward His Son: "I am pleased with you, my favor rests on you, and my delight is in you." Paul Countinho echoed, "What matters is not if people say good or bad things about me; what matters is the way I feel in my relationship with God and that I am free."[13] Jesus does not build his happiness around, or find meaning for His life in, what people think about Him, but in what His Father thinks and feels about Him.

The one who is truly saved by grace knows the cross accomplished far more than showing God's love. Jesus' blood poured out points to a deeper truth: you cannot accomplish for yourself what God has already done for you. Jesus took on himself all of our sin and eliminated it. When our sin is removed, something else is revealed from underneath. We see the beggars we really are.

The cross haunts the one who experiences the heart that is left beating beneath the machine. "Jesus, are you crazy? Why did you have to die?" The answer is found in knowing God loved the world so very much that He gave his only Son to die, that whoever would believe in him would have eternal life. The answer is found in knowing God loved you so much that He delivered himself up for you. Love is the reason. Love is why Jesus had to die.

Stop for a moment, because I realize you know John 3:16. Stop for a moment, because I know it is easy to just paint the word LOVE over the story of the cross. Stop for a moment, because I know we can watch movies and listen to songs about two lovers' willingness to do wild, preposterous things to express their unrelenting love for the other, but we get fluffy on our connectedness when we start to talk about the absurdity of the love displayed for us on the cross.

The heartbeat beneath the broken machines of our own construction forces us to burst with adoration. When we break down all the shiny pieces we have put in place, we can see that we have been given forgiveness that warrants gratitude. We repent *because* we have been forgiven, not *so that* we could be forgiven. This requires a great amount of trust.

The one saved by grace in practice and theory lives in trust. You have to be willing to risk your reputation to fully trust the restoration project God has enacted in your life. You have to know you are loved by the Father and be free from what others might think about you. "To trust Abba, both in prayer and life, is to stand in childlike openness before a mystery of gracious love and acceptance."[14] This is an enormous act of trust and love that is necessary of a person who seeks to engage the heart beneath the machine.

Do you really believe that God is gracious, that He cares about you personally? Do you really believe He is always, reliably, present to you as a friend and encouragement? Can you say you actually believe God is love?

For many of us, a new sort of relationship is needed with our Father. You need a relationship that drives away all your fear, shame, and guilt. If your life of faith is not one that is abundant and full (John 10:10), you are missing the heart of the gospel. If you do not know an intimacy with God, and you are constantly asking for God to give you a vision, a sign, or a miracle, you may not know what it means to fully trust the gospel of grace.

Trust is required of you. The gospel demands of you a confidence that says, "Father, when I look at Jesus, I know you love me. I know you have forgiven me. I know you will hold on to me, and you will never let me escape you. I trust you!"

This humility is a foundation many of us do not understand. When my girls make fun of themselves or each other, I am learning to enter those moments immediately and say, "You will not talk about my daughter like that! It is not okay with me to hear you speak about my daughter in that fashion." I have known a dreadful number of Christians who self-defeat and call it "humility." The gospel does not heap more guilt and shame onto you; how dare you break yourself down and call it "humility"?

We have a tendency to build our machines to look

wonderful to those around us. We come to be quite proud of the faith we build for the eyes of other people. When life presses in on our machine faith and breakage happens, we are so distressed to see what we built destroyed. "We are appalled by our own inconsistency, devastated that we have not lived up to our own lofty expectations of ourselves."[15]

There is a great value to self-examination within our day-to-day walking with Christ. It is why the psalmist prayed, "Search me, O God, and know my heart! Try me and know my thoughts! And see if there be any grievous way in me, and lead me in the way everlasting." (Ps. 139:23–24). When we do the necessary work of self-examination we must invite God to search along with us and reveal what things He will. We do this because, when left to our own, we have two primary tendencies, both of which are destructive to the honest heart after God.

My first tendency is to praise myself too highly. If I do not ask God to search and reveal my heart, I will make excuses for every wicked or troublesome thing in my heart and mind. I will make light of dark things that ought to be dealt with.

My other tendency is to blame myself too heavily. If I do not ask God to search and reveal my heart, I will tirelessly break myself down. For some of us, God is entirely more gracious toward our sin than we would ever dream of being for ourselves. This is why we need God to search and reveal our true heart's condition.

God is fully aware of our tendency toward one of these extremes (I more often find myself in the latter). Because He is aware of our tendency, and because He knows that too much self-examination does more harm than good, He presents in the Psalms how we ought to search and reveal the sin in our lives. We go about this with humility and grace, and only God can accomplish that balance—between the extremes of praise and blame—with perfection.

We are powerless to repair ourselves, and in fact, we have a tendency to break down our own machines. The moment we realize and accept that we are powerless to repair our own brokenness is the point where we can begin to see the goodness of the gospel. When we start to really grow in the gospel, we realize how broken and poor we really become, and that realization is a great gift. This is what Jesus meant when he told us to be poor in spirit.

When you live in this way, you influence others on a much deeper level as well. Your poverty of spirit allows you to notice others and be able to enter into their lives with more grace than those who believe they are better than others. Can you look at your flawed life and make peace with its reality? You do not love your sin, but you also do not excuse it. Can you simply accept that it is your sin that provided the very need for the mercy God showered on you?

When you come to worship on a Sunday morning, you have to bring your best. In the Old Testament, God gives a lot of rules for the sacrifices to be brought before Him. He would tell the Israelites to bring a bull, and it had to be the best bull. If they did not have a bull, they were to bring a ram, and it must be the best ram. God's requirements for sacrifices went all the way down to at least a quail. If all an Israelite family had was a quail, bring it, but it must be the best quail. The person who encounters the gospel on a heart level can come to worship on a Sunday morning saying, "I do not have as much in me as I had last week, but today I choose to bring you my best."

Our relationship with anyone is good when both people desire for the other person to be happy and pleased with the relationship. At our deepest heart level, I am convinced this is where our connection to the heart of Jesus thrives. We want each other to be delighted. This means when you pray in silence, you do not cease to pray. It means when you flub your attempts to be loving, compassionate, peaceful, and good, God picks you up in his arms to say, "I understand!"

But we are not so content with this grace, are we? We cannot meet Paul in his declaration: "For the sake of Christ, then, I am *content* with weaknesses, insults, hardships, persecutions, and calamities. For when I am weak, then I am strong." (2 Cor. 12:10, emphasis mine). Would I be so content with these things? I am not wondering, as I normally do, whether or not I would *accept* these things, but would I really be *content* with them? The true heart of reliance on God's strength is far more than accepting these things; rather, it is being truly content in and through them.

In a final interview for a position as Community Care Pastor for a drop-in center, I was given some context for the guests at that center. The interviewer adopted a particular tone to check if I was okay with the center's regular guests, saying, "Our lobby does not always smell great." I remember thinking to myself, "Great! That is the smell of brokenness, and I am comfortable with brokenness." You can only be comfortable in the presence of brokenness if you have truly encountered grace in your most broken places.

In Christ, God became one with our brokenness.

You see it in the clay. If you have ever worked with clay, you know it is weak and imperfect. It has no real structure or integrity of its own. We have come from the dirt that makes up the clay, and God becomes one with our broken humanity in the Incarnation.

Now here is the good news: God knows and never forgets we are made of clay. You see Him interact with all the fathers of faith in the Old Testament, men who were liars, immoral, weak, and sinful were still blessed by God. How can you know if your God is the God of Abraham, Isaac, and Jacob? If your God is intimate with you, then this is your God. If you can accept yourself in your brokenness and experience God's love in your weakness, imperfection, and sinfulness, then your God is the same whose heart beats for you.[16]

If, on the other hand, you are content with God loving you unconditionally and you do not reach out to other broken people, then your god may not be the God of the gospel of grace. When you see others' imperfection and filth, you have to remember those people are also made of clay. They are also weak, bedraggled, and in need of the same mercy that has been lavished on you.

I, for one, would really like to thank you for being the worst sinner, because for a long time I thought I was the worst. Wait! Nope! I am *still* the worst sinner. You are welcomed to take second place if you would like, but I am the worst. Thank you very much.

I am not as bad as you think I am; I am much worse.

Paul tells me I am the worst of sinners so that mercy may be shown to others through Jesus Christ (1 Tim. 1:15-16). People quote that verse and forget it is only possible if they realize they are sinners who actually *need* mercy. You do not *deserve* mercy; you *need* mercy.

If you do not accept this detail, you have no need for Jesus at all. My constant striving for a perfect standard shows how little I believe my need for Jesus. This is not only where the gospel begins; it is where we ought to begin in our presentation of the gospel.

I wonder how much more the gospel would be heard and received if we presented it like Paul does in 1 Timothy. What if our communication of the gospel began and continued with the strong understanding that "I am the worst of sinners" instead of "You are the worst of sinners"? We are so quick to assume certain sins are worse than our own. I am quick to label others' sins as *abominations* while overlooking the long list of abominations listed in Scripture, many of which I find myself committing plenty of times in a day or week.

When was the last time someone said to you, "Let me tell you about those Christians—they are fantastic listeners. I have never seen a group of people more interested in knowing about my life with curious questions—people who really listen to me!" What a great question we all know the answer to! We know Christians have a bad rap when it comes to the way they treat people. But the real bad news is if we are honest, most of our rap sheet speaks the truth.

What will it take for us to be better lovers of people, showing grace and mercy to Christians and non-Christians alike? We have to learn how to enter into another person's world. We have to learn how to really listen. I have taken so many classes that, at some point, stressed listening skills. I don't know that I can count how many role-playing exercises I have done in classes and trainings. I don't know how many times I have done these things, and yet I still listen so poorly.

Think of the moments you wanted to be listened to most. A lot of those times were when I struggled through my faith. I was rarely asking for advice. I longed for people to join me and see how difficult the world looked from my lonely shoes.

Christians are not known to be very good listeners, and the further they get into ministerial leadership, the worse they can get at listening. The further I get in Christian leadership, the more I learn, and thus the more advice I can give you. The problem with that is our title and advancement in ministry does not result in automatic maturing in other areas. We can acquire all kinds of spiritual gifts and maturity and still be a bunch of babies (1 Cor. 3). We have to dive into ourselves and know more about who we are and who God is forming us to become, but we also must be willing to enter into others' situations. This is how we love more.

In the last few decades, I have been given many opportunities to speak, teach, and preach. I recognize how much grace I have been given to speak God's word. To preach is grace! To preach the gospel is amazing grace! I sat thinking of the enormous gift I have been given to do something that is truly worship for those wired in a similar fashion as me. I started to wonder what people walk away with after our time together. These are my reflections:

If I am preaching, I want the ragamuffin pilgrim in me to be palpable. I want it to be clear and obvious that I sit beside those in the pews, never standing above them. I am as bedraggled and beat up as you on any given day. I am also walking the straight and narrow, which just happens to also be rugged and beaten. My friends, we are still on the right path.

When I preach or stand before a group of people, I hope and pray they recognize a ragamuffin man who loves God and people with honest passion. I want them to see a man who, once he came to Jesus, he kept coming to Jesus. I hope that before them is seen a man stretching out his hand to touch the hem of Jesus' garment from fear that I am too unclean to embrace Him as fully as I would like.

Yes, they hear me saying things; but the question really is, "What is God trying to say through my stumbling rhetoric?" I am a culprit among culprits. I hope my sermons and books would not come across as disembodied parts. If I ever step in front of people as one "who dwells with God in light accessible," I would hope to never do this again. May I always share in some way the poverty of the poor in spirit! I want to speak in such a way of the ludicrous love of God that others cannot help but think, "Wow! He really believes this stuff!"

BOO BOO BUDDIES AND DADDY, I LOVE YOUS

EVERYTHING YOU DO comes out of your beliefs about yourself, others, and God. By this I mean that everything you do, every action, has a root in some belief you have about yourself, our world, or your God. Our belief system is a foundation because it is from there we act.

Why? It's because our beliefs create emotions, and our emotions drive a great deal of our behaviors.

We have to examine our beliefs in order to change and heal. Now, by "beliefs" I am not talking about proofs. We have to dig deeper into our hearts to see what we really believe about ourselves, our world, and our God. I do not mean to speak about indoctrinated, stale answers. I mean we have to answer, with 100% honesty, questions like:

> Do I believe God loves me tenderly?
> Do I believe I can know God personally?
> Is God a force, a character, a person, or something else?
> Do I believe I am a child of God?
> Do I believe I am worthy of love?
> Can anyone be trusted?
> Is it worth the risk to trust new people?

If I have been hurt, should I trust anyone ever again?
Are all people hurtful?
Can God really heal me and love me?

The questions go on and on, but these are good starting points for us to examine our belief systems if we truly desire healing and change in our lives. Change is going to require insight into and engagement with our deep-seated beliefs about self, others, and God. These beliefs drive our attitude toward ourselves, others, and God. That attitude in turn triggers our behaviors and actions.

> What comes in our minds when we think about God is the most important thing about us. For this the gravest question before the Church is always God himself, and the most portentous fact about any man is not what he at a given time may say or do, but what he in his deep heart conceives God to be like.[17]

We have an entire gallery of images within our heart and soul from which our conceptions of God come. Our images, or impressions, of God are critical to our spiritual well-being. The problem is many of those images are distorted. We have taken different experiences, circumstances, and relationships and projected them onto our image of God. Many of these are distortions of who God is.

The images of God we hang in our heart's gallery influence us mightily. They are more influential than our doctrines and ideas about God. They are more influential because these images are rooted in a deeper place where emotional experiences have taken place.

It is important that we recognize these distortions. They interfere with our ability to trust or speak with God. However, Christians are not the only ones with distorted images of God. In fact, those who do not believe in God, when asked to describe God, commonly offer portrayals of a god you likely do not believe in either. These distortions are common in the heart of humankind, Christian or not.

I played football for several years into high school. I started and played up until my senior year of high school, when I decided to quit. Playing football was no longer as enjoyable and thrilling for me as it once was. I had also played trumpet for about nine years. I was the first-chair trumpet player until senior year. I loved concert band, but I hated marching band. But since I played football, I never had to march. Once I decided to quit playing football, I realized, "Wait a minute! Now I have to do marching band." So I quit band too.

When I quit, my biggest concern was telling my grandfather of my decision. He was one of the most prominent male figures in my life at the time, and I wanted him to be proud of me. I was concerned he would be disappointed. Once I mustered the courage to break the news to him, he disarmed my anxiety. He said he was always going to be proud. If I wanted to quit, that was fine with him.

Kids crave approval from the primary adults in their lives. More than crave it, they *need* the encouragement and approval. Unfortunately, more often than not parents withhold encouraging words from their kids. Some parents spend more time criticizing and correcting their kids than they do encouraging (if at all).

You may have had this experience, whether you played

sports or not. Perhaps it was the experience of trying to please parents for whom nothing seemed good enough. You could have given a game-winning performance, but there would be something about your stance, or your swing, or *something* that was not good enough.

And the criticism and the pressure to perform does not end at little league and childhood performance, does it? Perhaps you go to college and work hard for a degree that simply is not the one your parents wanted you to pursue. You do not fulfill their expectations of you. You could have graduated *summa cum laude*, but since you are not a doctor, a nurse, a teacher, or whatever they wanted you to be, it simply is not enough.

It becomes impossible to win your parents' approval. Nothing is ever enough. So you convince yourself that it is impossible to make them happy. You are convinced there is no possible way you could meet their expectations.

If these scenarios resonate with your experiences, it is only natural that you would project on to God the impression that nothing would ever been good enough for Him. All of the sudden, God becomes full of impossible expectations. He is impossible to please. You crave and desire his approval and closeness, but how could it ever be possible to get that approval if nothing you do is ever enough? A distorted image has made its way into your heart's gallery.

Both physical and verbal violence leaves someone feeling terrified, violated, and—ultimately—unsafe. It feels like there is nowhere to hide.

Do you ever sense that God is only angry, waiting for you to mess up so He can punish you with harsh things you could never withstand? Does it seem like God is incredibly easy to anger, and you live your faith on pins and needles hoping not to upset Him? Does He seem overly demanding and does he seem to be waiting to punish you for your inability to meet impossible demands? Do you sometimes feel like you are unlovable, incapable, and of no value to God?

Separation, divorce (parents' or your own), death, or endless hours your caretakers spent away is all abandonment. When someone we depended on leaves, we are abandoned and we lose a sense of security or stability. There is nothing or no one there to rest or depend on. This is the image of abandonment.

There is a sense of guilt that comes with abandonment. We will often believe that it was our fault that people we depend on leave us. We start a lot of our thoughts with, "If I had only...." We feel a sense of responsibility. We might become really fearful and worry that other people are going to do the same thing, so we refuse to depend on or trust anyone else. Or we do everything we can to impress that person who abandoned us. We think, "Maybe, just maybe, if I'm good enough I can keep them around or make them come back."

Like all the other distorted images we have mentioned, we project that image onto God. I cannot trust God or depend on God because He will leave me. He will abandon me like everyone else, and I risk getting hurt if I trust Him now. Or perhaps I will do whatever I can to impress Him so He won't leave me. All of a sudden, God becomes a God who abandons, but that is an incredibly distorted image of God.

This chapter does not warrant the subtitle of "Daddy Issues," but that being said,...my dad...loves me, and I realize that. My parents have been divorced since before I was old enough to remember them married. Growing up with my mom, I remember my dad as not only physically distant, but also emotionally distant. Even on visits with dad, I found it a struggle to relate to him on an emotional level. There has been a very minimal emotional connection between my dad and me, and we still wrestle with that distance today.

As a junior in college, I met with a mentor for lunch, and our discussion turned to the topic of prayer. He asked me if I had a hard time addressing God as Father because of my history. I had to admit that I did have a difficult time addressing God as my Father. I remember a missionary who came to our university a few times from Papua New Guinea. She referred to God as "Papa God" in her prayers. I remember thinking that was an awesome way of addressing God, but I had never had an emotional connection in that area to really relate to God in that way. Again, a distorted image has made its way into my soul's gallery, and I have allowed that to affect my image of God.

From the time we were children we have needed our feelings to be acknowledged and responded to. We have a need for our emotions to be understood by others, especially those who are in any sort of authority over us. If not recognized, our emotions are discounted and minimized, and that creates distance between us and those we need emotional validation from. Two people in the same room can be a world apart emotionally. There is a great shame when you sense that your emotions do not matter to someone else. But we need to know and embrace the fact that our sadness, happiness, frustration, hurt, and pain matter.

When we project a distorted image onto God—one that depicts God as unsympathetic, distant, cold, and unapproachable—we begin to understand Him as emotionally distant, incapable of intimacy, and too busy. But we are not the first to believe this lie. The Stoic philosophers argued that God is unable to feel, because if He could, He would be capable of being influenced. The Epicurean said God is detached, unaware, and disconnected. Even the Jewish people struggled with putting an extreme focus on God's holiness—He is separated from sin, and thus incapable of sharing in human experience. Then Jesus came with a groundbreaking message about a transcendent God with immanent empathy who can be trusted *because* He feels. Still, we find ourselves wrestling with the same issue when we wonder, "How could God understand my problem? Does he even care about what I feel?"

These distortions will never be repaired or healed by just wishing them away. You cannot just cover them up, as we typically do. When you cover something up, it still remains. The only way to find healing from these distorted images is to *replace* them with the truth. The Father stands before our distortion and says to us, "Don't ever be so foolish as to measure my love for you in terms of your love for me! Don't ever compare your thin, pallid, wavering, and moody love with my love, for I am God, not man."[18]

We need to consider some important questions when we want to tackle these distorted images. What image of God was presented to me as a child? When did that image change, or has it ever changed? Who is God to me now? What is a deeper expression of my relationship with God going to look like after today? I need to have answers for these questions.

Regardless of what you have learned or projected on

to God, you have to make room for the infinite God. You cannot cram the infinite God into your rigid machinery. He will break every constraint you build, and it will leave a great deal of rubble to sort through. You must be ever cognizant of the need to revisit and adjust your image of God, according to the Scriptural truths, not your own experiences. But what about His image of you?

I have served as a pastor at a ministry to those who are homeless, addicted, and in other environments of crisis. In a group session the other day, a resident searched out the belief system that led to a decision she had made. Her self-image was poor, and her image of God was poorer. It was asked of her, "What do you think God felt toward you in that moment?" After a fumbling dance around the question she still couldn't answer it. So I asked her again. She could not experience the reality that God actually feels something toward her in the moments of her life.

Can you imagine God loving you just as irrationally as the lovers we see in Hollywood narratives? Love is often very irrational. It is blind to mistakes and red flags. It can be terribly jealous and furious. Can you see the image of God growing when you allow for it to include emotion and expression toward you as the object of His desire?

When we are sinking in over our head and treading water, we want to ask God, "How deep is your love? How great is your love really going to be for me?" John asks and answers the same question in one of the most affectionate verses in all of Scripture. "How great is the love the Father has lavished on us that we should be called children of God, and that is what we are." (1 John 3:1)

The Holy Spirit is the most prominent character in chapter 8 of Romans. The word *spirit* occurs 18-19 times depending upon the translation, which is 60% of all references to the word in the whole book of Romans. The Holy Spirit's action within us is incredibly important because it is in contrast to our natural and sinful self.

The Spirit within us is active and speaking to us at our very core, but what is it saying? If you are a Christian, you have within you a Spirit that cries out "Abba Father," as verse 15 says. Understand this: at the very core of who you really are is a heart and Spirit that is crying out Abba Father.

This tender connection with the heart of God is at your very core. Your spirit, your heart, you inner being cries out Abba Father, because your spirit understands you are a child of God. Your very core, your spirit knows itself as the beloved child of God. Being the beloved child of God is the very core of your existence; it is who you are. At your core, no matter what other things you use to define yourself, you are God's beloved, His child.

But there is a problem, isn't there? There is within us a voice that cries out Abba Father, a core inner being who understands himself as the child of God, who knows herself as the beloved, but that Spirit is silenced by all the other things we use to define ourselves. My spirit cries out Abba Father, but when I allow other people and my past to eclipse that cry, I grow spiritually dead, and the machine takes the heart. Although my spirit is designed to cry out of this one thing, this belovedness, it grows faint and dead when I drown it out with all other things.

There are always new ways to identify my inner Pharisee shadowing my inner child of God. I recognized this in watching my children. Their expression of emotion is enormous and spontaneous. My girls have the capacity to move to drastic stages in emotional expression out of nowhere. It only takes a statement from me or anyone else, and my girls will jump right in to the pool of emotion with no abandon.

A part of me identifies those emotional outbursts as dramatic and unreasonable. This part of me is the inner Pharisee, but you and I like to call it "maturity" and "adulthood." We can become irritated by the outbursts of children and their big feelings, but that irritation is because we have come far enough down a line of Pharisaic maturity, devaluing the expression of emotion. The Pharisee in me says, "You have got to learn to get over this. You have to let these things roll off you, because life is going to be hard." My inner Pharisee says, "Grow up and stop whining!"

Contrary to this, my inner child of God knows how to open myself to other people and refuses to lie about my loneliness, sadness, insecurity, and fear. My inner child hears my girls' outbursts and identifies with them entirely. The inner child screams to me, "Hey! You have fears and hurts and affections too! You just quit listening to them."

The moments I open myself to Abba and share how much they mean to me are moments when the child of God wins over the Pharisee. These are moments the Holy Spirit reveals the deepest work in the child of God. But it is important to know these moments are not always what we expect.

The desert temptations of Jesus in Matthew 4 all add up to the same question: "If you are the Son of God...." How interesting that Satan would be using the question immediately after the Father had already stated by the Jordan River that Jesus *is* His son! Immediately after God declares the truth of Jesus' identity, Satan comes and launches an attack on that identity. Does Jesus believe strongly enough who the Father says He is?

Does Jesus not only trust who God says He is but also fully embrace His identity as the Son?

Something happens in the wilderness, and our identity is at risk. In the desert times of life we are interpreters of something vital. Our wilderness moments are often immediately after we have been confident of who we are. So we enter a desert moment when an enemy will attack our identity and challenge our trust and embrace of what God has already said of who we are.

We are not as trusting and confident as our Lord. Not all of us are strong enough to emerge from our desert moments in life with a full trust in our identity as sons and daughters of God. There are still voices that haunt the child of God in the wilderness, urging you to "prove to myself and others that I am worth being loved, and they keep pushing me to do everything possible to gain acceptance."[19] Some are able to stand in the wilderness and know they live on every word from the mouth of God. But few are so firmly rooted in their identity as sons and daughters of God that they can stand confidently in the face of this question in the wilderness.

This has been the challenge of every wilderness that God's children journey through: "If you are a son or daughter of God...." When faced with that question, you need to trust and embrace the identity your Father has already spoken over you. That is who you are.

As a father of two daughters, I've always thought I might kill the first person to convince my daughter she was ugly, unlovable, worthless, or anything against what I know her to be. Do you know you have a Father who has spoken very clearly who you are as His child and is prepared to stand against anyone or any thing or any force that would convince you otherwise?

The inner child knows God loves him, and if he is not cultivated and sustained, the Christian's mind slowly closes to new opinions, nonpaying obligations, and the awe of the Spirit's work. Once a mind closes to this level, it kills relationships, numbs away feelings and sympathies, and makes for a church full of deadbeats. If the inner child is sustained, however, there is open-mindedness that breeds iconoclasts who are willing to challenge set structures and ideas, including their own.

The children of God are not content to be who they are not. The gospel is not for pretenders and liars, even when the lie is one you believe about yourself. The kingdom that Jesus describes is for those who are not pretending to be cleaner than they are. It is for the ones smart enough to know how foolish they are. You belong to this kingdom. This is a kingdom for those who are free, because no greater freedom is felt than when a person does not incessantly attempt to sustain a false identity for everyone else to believe.

One of the most difficult things for me as a father of young daughters is handling their frustration. My five-year-old is learning to express her feelings and thoughts, but she has begun using words she likely hears at school. In the last couple of years, the words *fat* and *ugly* have come into her vocabulary, and nothing angers me more when my girls use those words against each other or themselves.

In case you glossed over the details above, my 5 year

old talks about being fat and ugly. The first time she said the word *fat*, I pulled the car over to the side of the road as if she had said the other F-word. I pulled to the side of the road because that is what you do when your child says something so terribly inappropriate and hurtful that it must be dealt with right away.

"Bryleigh, I do not want to hear that word come out of your mouth again. Do you understand me?"

I realize self-image is going to be an issue for the rest of my life as I raise girls and live in a house full of them. I understand, to some degree, it comes with the territory. But I also understand how much of that trouble comes from the environment we facilitate in our home. I understand a father's words mean a universe to his daughters. I hate these words, and it angers me to hear them in my home from the mouths (and hearts) of my girls.

The god many of us relate to is not the God of Scripture, and we begin to wonder why so many live out such a grim, hard, and loveless faith each day. It is because the god we have come to believe is distant and hard to please. God becomes a cold Father demanding your work without encouragement or love or pride in you. It is very difficult to serve that god with enthusiasm or joy because it is hard to serve a machine. It is difficult not to chalk up other more enthusiastic brothers and sisters to fanaticism when the god you know is cold, removed, and grim. But this is not the God presented in Scripture. This is the god of the Pharisees who will always drive a mechanical religion and faith.

The moment I was first ensnared by the love of God was when I came to see God as the Father of Scripture who loves and delights in me, His son. He comes close to me in a true fellowship where I can find rest and healing. He is not hard to please. I have come to know His delight and His smile. He will correct and challenge me with the smile of a Father who is tender and proud. My Abba is proud of me and knows I am His imperfect but promising son. I see His delighted smile; He knows I am becoming to look more and more like my Abba every day.

When the child of God believes the Spirit in himself who bears witness that he is a child of God, "and if children, then an heir—heir of God and fellow heir with Christ," (Rom. 8:17) he knows the weight of this blessing. It is a birthright. The gifts we experience in the gospel of God's love are not privileges; they became a birthright when you became a child of God.

The gospel is for the sin-soaked and the broken who are loved and outspoken. It is for the ones who realize *unworthy* and *worthless* are not the same things. There is a great difference, and the child of God does not have time to waste in believing she is worthless. She knows she does not deserve the love of her Father, but she knows her Father gives her great value. She is a child of a King.

As you finish reading this chapter, stop for a moment and take a breath. It has been proven that human beings only use a fraction of our lungs' capacity each day because we breathe so shallowly. We also know that oxygen in our bloodstream gives us energy and life. So take a large breath, fill your lungs and stomach, release it and read this from your Father:

Child,

I am not here to speak to you. You are not here that I might teach you something. I ask you to rest right now. Be silent and quiet. I do not ask you to do this so you may *do* anything else. I am not going to speak to you. I merely ask that you are silent and just…let…me…love…you. Be still and drink in my love. Do not sit and think too heavily *about* my love. Just sit quietly in my lap with your head on my chest and let me love you.

My love is not an ideal or a theology to study. My love, right now, is my action. I am loving you. Be still in my arms and let me love you. Be still and drink in the love that radiates from me into you right now, waiting to fall upon your silence, your stillness. If you are not still, you will only rustle it about. But if you are still, my love will pour upon you like snow in a globe. You can be covered in my love, but you must be still and allow me to rain down on you more love than you will ever be able to contain.

Don't think! Don't listen for me! For I have nothing to say to you right now! I only have something to give you. I have only to love you right now. Rest and be loved, my wonderful child.

FAINT SHADOWS AND TOO MUCH LIGHT

THE STORY IS told of a man who would drink himself into a blackout at a local bar and stumble back to his home nearly every night. One of these nights, he came home and vomited on the kitchen floor. His wife had finally had enough, and she called the pastor, who came over immediately.

They carried the man to his bedroom and tucked him in. The pastor began a quiet prayer, "Lord, as you look upon this sloppy drunk..."

The man interrupted the prayer and slurred out the request, "Don't tell Him I'm drunk! Tell Him I'm sick!"

We are stupid people, are we not? We are convinced that we can hide things from God with a wink and a white lie. Perhaps people can be hoodwinked, but God knows us, with all our shadows and scuffles.

Each day, the first people I see call me "Daddy." I begin my day as "Dad." Another person calls me "Babe" (which I realize is the furthest cry of my day). I then commute to a place where some people call me "Pastor." I am defined as a shepherd who sits with broken people for a moment and gives care in various fashions. Many weekends, I get the grace to travel and speak at various events, churches, and groups. There is a particular lens through which people see the speaker and author PC Walker.

Is it any wonder that at the end of a day or week, I might look in the mirror and ask, "Just who in the world do you really think you are?" I play so many parts for different people; it is easy to be puzzled as to who I really am.

It can be quite difficult to remember the solution is truly found in allowing Jesus to define who I am. When I am honest, I know I would be lost if any of these identities were stripped from me. I know because many of them *have* been stripped from me at different moments in my life.

Something within us seeks to protect and present the best image of ourselves for others to see. Brennan Manning calls this "the Imposter." Others have called it the false self or the shadow side. It always rises and falls on the approval or disapproval of other people. This part of us is forged in childhood, when for some reason we were not loved the way we ought to have been. Whatever the cause of our tendency toward it, the imposter is a liar.

My false self desperately wants to be liked and affirmed, and I come to a point where I believe the spiritual cosmetics I paint on myself. My imposter likes to ignore my loneliness and shallowness. I overlook the darkest corners of my messy life. I go into every day with a slight of hand to keep everyone focused on my shiniest attributes, even if I have to fabricate a few of them.

In E.B. White's classic children's tale *Charlotte's Webb*, the loveable protagonist, a little pig named Wilbur, befriends a spider that writes flattering words about Wilbur in her web. This does not only affect the onlookers; it also has an effect on Wilbur.

> Ever since the spider had befriended him, he had done his best to live up to his reputation. When Charlotte's web said SOME PIG, Wilbur had tried hard to look like some pig. When Charlotte's web said TERRIFIC, Wilbur had tried to look terrific. And now that the web said RADIANT, he did everything possible to make himself glow.[20]

This is the illusion of the imposter in each one of us. She wants to be noticed, and so she manipulates herself in any way to maintain the glowing image everyone wants to believe. The imposter has an appetite for approvals in order to be truly satisfied in life, but the sad irony is that the false self cannot know true intimacy in any relationship.

The narcissism of the imposter disregards others and makes it impossible to be known by anyone. He has no sense of real emotion, feelings, or sensitivity because they have all been numbed away by the façade of pleasantry. The imposter knows how to be social but is incapable of being relational. He cannot share himself, because he knows nothing true of himself.

The machine is made up primarily of imposter's ploys because the imposter specializes in replacing the heart with the beautiful machinery parts that everyone likes to see. This person the imposter wants me to be cannot actually exist, and it inevitably breaks down in faith because God does not know this false person. God only knows my true self.

We already discussed the fact that our belief system is a foundation in our lives and faith. We have to examine those beliefs in order to change and heal. Someone who believes deep down that their dad is smart, funny, and orderly but also believes he is a compulsive, insulting drunk is going to have to choose which of those beliefs will drive his emotions and behaviors toward his father.

People who believe they are not pretty, loveable, or worthy will begin to live their lives looking for someone else who will make them feel the opposite. Instead of changing the belief, they only attempt to fix the behavior to generate the praises they need to hear. One such person might say a friend "makes me feel loved, pretty, and of some worth." But in reality, neither person in that relationship is being healed in the heart.

Someone who believes God is a tyrant who awaits His next opportunity to punish the sinner would naturally act out against the idea of God. He will never be able to accept Christ. Someone who believes God would never love him as he is, "not with the things I have done," will never be able to live the Christian life of joy. He will never be able to truly worship or pray.

Once we begin to change our beliefs, we can begin to heal and step away from the behaviors and problems that have haunted and destroyed so much of our lives. It has to start with an address of the inward parts of our heart, soul, and spirit so God can walk us through our healing. Out of what is believed spiritually in the heart below the machine come our morals, values, relationships, and how we view ourselves and others.

In the environment I get to serve each day there is something called self-evaluation. Whenever someone in the house does something that needs a closer look, whether it was positive or negative, someone else in the house might say, "You're going to need to self-evaluate that at our next meeting." There is a form that the person who did the action would fill out and then talk it through with the rest of the house. The self-evaluation is a series of questions intended to explore the root of that action in depth. They ultimately lead to answering the question, "What belief inside me made me think that action was the right one in that moment?"

Here is our problem in life and faith. We are constantly trying to change our behaviors to just be better, but if we do not change the belief that gave birth to the behaviors, they will simply keep happening, no matter how much you want them to change. We have to let the gospel and God's word replace our false beliefs. If the beliefs do not change, there is no hope for your behaviors or life to ever change.

This means when you look at yourself, you need to ask what you really, at your core, believe about yourself.

And what does the gospel say about you?

There is a social psychological concept called the "looking-glass self," which essentially theorizes that we become more and more what the most important person in our life thinks we are. In life there are many people who have different perceptions of who we really are. Exes are going to have a different perception of you from your momma. Coworkers are going to have different perceptions of you from your spouse.

The looking-glass self will often so strongly believe these perceptions that we actually become the person that the most important person in our life perceives us to be. This brings up a couple of very important questions. First, who is the most important person in my life (and why is it not the Father)? Before I answer, I realize we give certain people importance in our lives. Moreover, the most important person in our lives is not always the most "positive-impact" person in our life. For many of us the most important person in their life might be the abusive parent or spouse, and that significantly mangles our self-perception.

You may give too much importance to the person you are dating, who perceives you only as someone who makes him feel good. You begin to believe you are only exactly that, and you tear yourself down with shame when he says you are worthless and will never be loved.

If you are a follower of Jesus, this first question—who the most important person is in your life—necessarily leads to a second question: Why is it not God? Of course we may say He is, but theory is different from practice. Can you honestly say your relationship with Jesus is the most important relationship you have and maintain? Can you say that God's perception of you *is* who you really are, or are you really becoming who some other person perceives you to be, someone to whom you have given more importance than the Father?

If God is the most important person in my life and my relationship with Jesus is the most important relationship I have, then the next questions to answer is "Who *does* God perceive me to be?"

"We even refuse to be our true self with God—and then wonder why we lack intimacy with Him."[21] Psalm 73:28 makes clear that our deepest desire is to be close to God. We yearn for that intimacy, because it is what we are made for. There is nothing in this life that could ever fulfill us in the same way.

But the imposter is not comfortable with this sort of intimacy. "No one told me that when I wear a mask, only my mask receives love."[22] The Imposter specializes in veneer and will put forth whatever good-looking face he can in order to avoid the real effort of intimate connection. Appearances are always going to undermine reality for the imposter.

An intimate relationship with the heart of Jesus exists between the quest for honesty and authentic personality, but the false self is far too cowardly to swim here. "Those who are so absolute in their assertions and reproaches to others are seeking, without being fully aware of the fact, to reassure themselves. They rid themselves of their own doubts by awakening doubt in others."[23] Honesty and transparency are flickering flames in the dark holes where the imposter slithers about.

It was so easy to be angry with legalistic Christians who have no idea what it means to love in this way. But I quit being angry and bitter when I made a guess at why they were so poor at loving although God had called us to love others as we love ourselves.

It appeared to me that perhaps we Christians struggle to love others because we do not actually know how to love ourselves. For so many of us, or I know at least for me, I would not wish on anyone the kind of "love" I dish out on myself much of the time. So I see Christians in a different light. We are terrible at loving others because we do not know how to love ourselves as Christ sees and loves us. So the cycle begins.

Another point in this cycle answers the question, "Why do we struggle to love ourselves?" Why do Christians have such a horrible time loving themselves and thus loving and accepting others?

The answer comes from within the question. It is because we have been hurt by the imposter cycle.

I have a hard time loving and accepting others because I have a hard time loving myself, and I have a hard time loving and accepting myself because I do not feel loved and accepted by Christians, and Christians have a hard time loving and accepting me because they have a hard time loving and accepting themselves. They have a hard time loving and accepting themselves because I, a Christian, have a hard time loving and accepting them. This cycle thickens by the day, and I am more a part of it than I ever realized.

Can the cycle be broken? Yes!

How?

If I learn to love and accept myself as I am and others as they are, the cycle could break. It requires that I stop withholding love and acceptance. The easiest cycle breaker (and hardest personal choice) is to break the cycle at my own point of reality and brokenness. It happens in the wilderness. "More than anything else, the wilderness purges us of our false self...because our false self is so entwined with our development, our relationships, our approach to life and our very personality, radical surgery is required to remove it from us."[24] That surgery takes place in the wilderness moments where we are forced to be honest.

I take away the pretense of perfection. Then I allow others to realize I have no pretended perfection of myself and I am able to have no pretended perfection of them. This will happen when I become more concerned with being honest and acquiring healing instead of appearing fine, okay, good, or—dare I say—perfect. It is in my brokenness that the imposter cycle is broken. Because it is then that I am able to love others as I love myself, by accepting myself despite my failures and mistakes. So when I love and accept others as I do myself, then they can love and accept themselves as they are, and then they can love others and me as they love themselves.

But for now, we actually *do* love others as we love ourselves...we fake and withhold our love!

There is nothing easy about looking into the eyes of the imposter. When you are face to face with the false self, you have to see the fear and darkness that lies there. "You've been a phony! Underneath all that fake stimulation you were scared to death and bitter and perhaps bored with life."[25] The truth lashes out from the depths where the imposter has held it captive. If you will sit and take an honest look at your imposter, the imposter cannot hide any longer.

Have you ever wondered why prayer seems to be such hard, unaffected work? Does it seem to you prayer is only the shuffle of memorized statements? If so, the imposter in you lingers on.

Mark 9:24 is one of my favorite verses in all of Scripture: "I believe; help my unbelief." It is so often the cry of my heart. I resonate with this verse more than others. I am always in a state of belief, and yet I am frequently in need of help for my unbelief.

Like the father in this story, at times I struggle to pray with enough fervency to claim that I am a man of real belief and faith. I struggle to pray for myself or others because a large part of me wanders into myriad questions. Then I wonder why anyone could pray with such fervency other than "because Jesus commanded us to do so."

But I know my faith is weak in moments, because by comparison, there are moments when prayer comes naturally. These are moments when I have such a clear glimpse of God that I hold on to it and squeeze every bit of life I can out of that moment. I need it to last as long as possible because I will drown in my own wandering thoughts again otherwise.

So to hear this man's plea with Jesus in Mark 9 is refreshing and affirming. It is affirming that this plea is granted and answered. It is affirming that even our admission of unbelief is more important and honorable to Jesus than when we simply do not get it but pretend we do. Those are the ones who are of "this faithless generation" (vs 19). Those are the ones who irritate Jesus for their lack of faith.

But you see Jesus encounter this father when he simply admits he does have faith but needs help in his lack of faith. Jesus meets you in that honesty. Sometimes we only need to pray and continue to pray to the God we only half believe in, and He will meet you tenderly and powerfully in return. *Or* you could remain part of the faithless generation that pretends we have all the faith in the world though there is no fruit to show for it.

I gave this same message to a group and received an anonymous letter afterwards:

> PC, I am a college student that is about to graduate, and I have been going through a brutally honest journey trying to figure out if I actually believe in God and Jesus like I thought I had my whole life. This Mark 9:14–29 passage you spoke about has been confusing for me, but on my heart for a few weeks now. I was affirmed when I heard about how God honors my honesty about my unbelief. This is what really encouraged me: [when you said] "Sometimes we only need to pray and continue

to pray to the God we only have believe in, and he will meet us tenderly in return." That is the cry of my heart right now. Last week, I realized I was only 50% sure God loved me, and it broke my heart. It bothers me so greatly to come to the realization that I am only 50% sure that there is even a God. But I will keep praying to the God I only half believe in, hoping He will kindly meet me in return, and help me become more sure of His love. Thank you, "Amanda."

I was never able to follow up to see when, and where, and how Jesus affirmed her honesty, but I trust that "Amanda" was met somewhere tenderly when she faced her imposter head on. She quit pretending that her mechanical faith was all she needed, and she admitted her lack of glitter and shine. Those are lonely places where the Father reveals His power and sends a torrential downpour of His love.

The imposter hates to be discovered. So it is no surprise that prayer is the hardest place to drag your imposter into. The imposter wants excitement and transcendence. "The false self is frustrated because he never hears God's voice. He cannot, since God sees no one there."[26] Prayer is so hard for the imposter because the imposter cannot encounter God.

The imposter must be called out. She has to be brought to the mat and exposed. But if you deny the existence of the imposter, it is impossible to heal from the lonely mechanical faith she wants to keep you built into. You will only move forward when you accept truth. You have to accept that you are broken and torn up enough to have needed an imposter to get you through to this point.

Do you see the key role of the imposter? For as long as the imposter exists within you, it threatens even the forgiveness that Jesus has for you. If I only pretend to be a sinner, I can only pretend to be forgiven. When I look at my confession of sin on a daily basis, how specific am I prepared to be? My imposter has no problem with confessing sin in general. He can confess he is a sinner all day, and he knows he is forgiven. The question has to be asked of me, "Forgiven for what?" Pretend sinners only receive pretend grace.

Be nice to yourself. You cannot hate the imposter, because—do not forget—the imposter is still entangled with you. Hating the imposter is only going to turn into self-hatred, and you will be no further than you were before you looked the imposter in the eye. The only way to heal is to accept that the only good thing about your sin is that it is what propels you to the grace and mercy of the Father. Sinfulness is a part of our real self, and you have to accept this.

I have to discover within myself who I really am and then give it over to Jesus. I have to let go of the constant craving for everyone else's approval of me. I have to let go of the fear that God dislikes me as much I dislike myself—because it isn't true.

The truth is, when I am in control of my own life, I end up being very destructive to myself and others. This is why it is very important for my life to be directed and controlled by God. The problem is I give control over to other things and people when I allow them to determine who I am. I realize in my mind these things and people cannot make me who I am intended to be, but I still find myself living differently. These things may change who I am on the outside, but they have nothing to do with who I really am. What I do comes out of who I am. How much do I realize God's love for me?

God loves me and cares for me. He has a plan and purpose for my life; all the other things I use to determine who I am are false. All the other things I have attached to my "self" are idols. I have attached my identity to other things than Christ and have, in so doing, created idols.

My true identity, who I really am, is God's beloved. I have to claim my identity solely with that realization. If I were able to do that perfectly, I would have given God complete control of my life.

We believe so many lies about ourselves, and when we believe those lies we develop different reactions to feel better about or forget about those lies. The terrible part of this whole thing is we are reacting to these lies. We have certain destructive behaviors, and we try to change the behavior without changing the lie that leads us to our behavior. In order for us to be better and whole (the real meaning of *shalom*), we have to identify and recognize the lies and false beliefs we have and how they affect us. Once we recognize the false beliefs, we can then replace them with truths.

Once we replace the lies with truth, we will find that our destructive behaviors, our under-reactions, and overreactions will also begin to change. Any situation in which I under-react or overreact to something involves some sort of pain, wound, or lie underneath the surface. I have protected my wounds with lies and false beliefs, and my behaviors have developed as a result.

In John 8, Jesus tells the Jews they are slaves to sin. But he tells them in verses 31–32 that if they would "continue in his word...and know the truth, that truth would make them free." We are slaves to our lies and false beliefs about ourselves. But if we would continue to listen to God's words and His heart for us, we would be able to see the truth about who we are, and that truth can set us free.

When Job expressed all his anger, pain, and frustration with God in the midst of his trouble, his friends gave some of the daftest advice (if you can call it "advice"). One of those things Eliphaz said to Job struck a blow to the imposter.

> What do you know that we do not know?
> What do you understand that we do not? (15:9)

If you pray honestly and relationally beneath the machine, others will wonder this very thing about you. I can remember September 11, as most people do. That night on my college campus, groups gathered to pray. I remember being in a circle of people and praying at one point. I do not recall the prayer specifically, but as we dispersed, some people came up to me to say, "I love the way you pray. You pray differently."

I did not understand why.

I have also had people in my life say things like, "You seem to relate to God so differently."

I do not do anything magical or especially revolutionary when I pray. In fact, most days I struggle to pray at all. But now when I do pray, I do so with honesty. I pray as I can and not as I can't. I pray and speak as if the Father listens to me, because I have come to trust that He does. My prayers are not memorized clichés. There are times when they are repetitive and terribly trite, but they are not clichéd phrases I have heard throughout my life. I do not talk to my friends in clichés, much less to my great Lover. What is interesting is when I do pray as I do or relate to God in this fashion, so many people around me begin to wonder:

> What do you know that we do not know?
> What do you understand that we do not?

I don't! I have not discovered anything that is hidden to others. I have only become convinced that God hears the honest prayers of relational sons and daughters who are convinced this is the only way.

Here is an added benefit to the authenticity that comes from a dissolving imposter; it allows you to treat others very differently. When you encounter the grace and mercy offered to your true self beneath the machinery parts your imposter built, you will give others a whole lot more grace. When I struggle to give grace to the broken and torn-up people in my life, I do not know grace as I say I do. I am frequently reminding myself so that I never forget just how far God had to stoop to rescue my disheveled heart.

A WARNING TO ALL THOSE WHO KNOW ME

My identity has been stolen! Be careful when you see "PC" because you need to determine whom you are actually speaking to. An imposter has stolen my identity, and the imposter is well liked and very crafty. He will do all he can to make you believe he is the real PC, but do not be fooled. The imposter looks a lot like me. Be on the lookout for a guy who looks just like me but may act or react in any variety of the following ways:

> He has no opinions of his own; he simply conforms. He acts "okay" when things are not okay. He lacks emotional honesty. He is overly anxious to impress you when he does not have to. He seems to be obsessed with getting you to like him. He will not tell you how he feels about... anything. He acts better than he really is (again, to impress you). He speaks very little about his faults, his struggles, or his friends and family. He demands to be noticed. He draws his identity from achievement, avoids feeling, and is overly passive. He also is just not creative at all; he is going to lack the creativity I have.

He may surface from time to time. If you notice this man, please report him to the proper authority. If you should come into contact with this imposter, please contact his Father (whose name is Abba) and be gentle. He is harmless to most people but me.

Has your identity been stolen by an imposter? What kind of person should I keep an eye out for?

THE WOBBLY AND WEAK-KNEED

SOMETHING WITHIN US wants to trust, does it not? Something within us would like to trust something or someone. But we simply don't! Why not?

We have been hurt before, haven't we? People have let us down in the past. Like machines, the thing about trust is that it also gets broken. Though we desperately want to trust, something with us just cannot manage to do so. People have hurt us. Things have not worked out, and we are singing along with the classic blues line, "IF it wasn't for bad luck, I wouldn't have no luck at all."

The invitation to trust invokes a voice within us that tells us not to, and that voice is called fear. But there is also another voice. Faint and distant, it says, "I am here. I am with you. I love you even now, even here. I am with you, and I will be with you when all things come and go."

We all hear this voice if we really listen. There is something within each of us who is broken and hurt that speaks this love to us. It does not matter if you are a Christian or not; we all want that voice to be true. We all want that voice to be real.

The issue of trust is at the core of what it means to engage the heart below the machine. But the truth is most of us struggle with trust. It is unnatural to us because we have a false perception of what trust really looks and acts like. We want to feel before we trust, but it simply does not work that way. We want to experience before we believe, but Jesus says, "that experience will not be given to you" (Matt. 12:39; Luke 11:29). Our expectations are not only unrealistic; they are unfaithful to a God who desires our unwavering trust.

You cannot wait to feel before you trust; it must go the other way.

To truly trust anything requires taking a risk. If you have not had to take a risk, you have not actually trusted someone or something. Trust is created in the soils of risk, not in the machinery of guarantees. In order for something to be risky, it has to come against a fear. Without fear nothing would be risky, and without risk you cannot trust.

We all want to be trusted, and God is no different. He desires to be trusted. What sort of demands do you put on that trust? If we do not take God at His word, take the risk and trust, we may never feel or experience God again.

Here is the thing about machines. Things happen on the outside, and machines cannot stand up to the pressure. Life happens, and a lot of Christians find themselves confronted with the broken pieces of the machines they had built strewn about their previously manicured life. For many of us, there are times our faith finds us in a place where we simply need God to steady our spinning head when the world around us is in a whirlwind. It would feel as though God had forgotten us in our greatest trouble. Many Christians for centuries have found themselves in that place.

I have a warning for you. If you commonly describe

your walk with Jesus as fine, good, or okay, if your prayers are timid, rehearsed, or respectful, you are in for a gut check as your engage this chapter. It is my intention to see you stirred.

We have created a culture that is foreign to lamenting prayers like the one found in Psalm 13. The Christian culture most of us grew up and even now live in is full of pleasantries and right answers. It is wracked with courtesy and good manners. Look at our popular music and books. We want it all to be positive and encouraging, safe for the whole family. Our Christian culture wants nothing unless it is pretty and purpose-driven. Everything is clean-cut, okay, fine, and good. But this tendency does not stop at our culture.

Our faith, prayers, and conversations have also become sterile, free of profanity and anger. But there are good reasons for this—we are called to think of things that are pure, noble, noteworthy, and excellent. I get that! I do!

But I also get it when it all hits the fan, and it does not seem to be getting better. I get it when Bible-verse-band-aids and Christian clichés do nothing to relieve the circumstances that obliterate all my earnest attempts at prayer.

We have created a culture where if you are not smiling, then you are not a believer. We have created a culture where if you are angry at God, you either fix it or pretend you are not, and you do it NOW! I've gotta say it's getting exhausting.

We like to read something like Psalm 13, because that faint voice in our heart is briefly soothed by the first part of that psalm before we quickly gloss it over. We want to get to the last part of the psalm as soon as we can. We want to get to the trust and the singing. We rush through the beginning in order to get to the hope and trust.

Not today!

I see despair. I see desperation. I see a frantic prayer of a person desperate for God to do something! If God is the only One who can do something about these things, why doesn't He do something?

David begins this psalm screaming! "How long, O LORD? Will your forget me forever? How long will you hide your face from me?" (vs. 1)

Can God forget anything? Who does David think he is to question God like this? How can he have the audacity to pray to God and say these words?

"Look at me!"
"Answer me!"
"Give light to my eyes!"

These are not formulaic prayers. We do not have cute little books in our bookstores based on this prayer. These are imperatives. They are demands David screams through gritted teeth. He is in the middle of the wilderness because he has been run off to escape someone he had served faithfully who now wants to kill him. He is left in the pain and wants to know how long.

"How long..." is the cry of David. "How long..." is the cry of the poor and broken who live in social systems that keep them there. "How long..." is the cry of the oppressed who cannot stand on their own lest they want to be beaten down further.

But "How long..." is also the cry of those who have sacrificed many things to follow the path God has placed them on only to feel forgotten in the wilderness. It is for those who chose a path that is straight and narrow but is also rugged and beaten. It is the cry of anyone of you whose bottom fell out long ago. "How long, God?!"

The end of the psalm may even catch us off guard. "But I have trusted in your steadfast love; my heart shall rejoice in your salvation. I will sing to the LORD, because he has dealt bountifully with me" (vv. 5-6). It seems such a sudden turn, perhaps too sudden, doesn't it? You have heard people say you just tell God you are mad, because He knows it anyway. That is true. Be honest! Pray honestly! Often when you pray honestly with your hurt and pain, God meets you there with change.

But sometimes He does not! The climax of this psalm is not "I will sing." The climax is not even "my heart rejoices." The climax of this psalm, the point that all the anguish, anger, and anxiety builds to is: "But I trust."

The Hebrew word used here for trust reveals completion. The words "sing" and "rejoice" actually reveal a sense of exerting David's will. It is as if to say "let me sing" and "let me rejoice." That means what is happening here is better served by an image of David gritting his teeth and telling his own heart, "Let me sing and rejoice though I do not particularly feel like it right now!" It is as if he is fighting within himself, saying, "God, even if you have forgotten me in my darkest hour, I will not forget you. I will not forget you told me I was your very own. I will not forget you have done many things for me in the past. Even though it feels like you have forgotten me, you will not leave me here. I do not know when you are going to come meet me here, but you will!"

Do you remember the story of Jacob wrestling with God in Genesis 32? They wrestled all night long until daybreak. Once the sun began to come up, God touched Jacob's thigh to cause a limp. Our poverty-stricken English language commonly refers to the location of God's touch as Jacob's hip. But it is a more accurate image to say the entire thigh was torn. God does this to Jacob and then says, "Let me go for the sun is coming up."

But Jacob held on!

He would not let go. He said, "I will not let you go unless you bless me."

God asks him, "What is your name?"

"Jacob!"

"No, you shall no longer be called Jacob, but Israel, for you have striven with God and with men, and have prevailed."

Psalm 13 is the cry of David, of Israel, and of you and me. It is a cry that says, "I will wrestle with God, with hope, with life, and I am not letting go until hope, until Life, until God meets me here and blesses me."

Wrestling is at the core of Christianity. There is a great paradox in the cross of Jesus. The empty tomb is beautiful, but it would not be there if it were not for the emptiness of the horrific cross. Though Jesus knew He would be raised from the dead, He still cried out in despair, "My God, My God, why have you forsaken me?" The same absurd wrestling match is expected of anyone who could call himself a follower of Jesus.

It is a legacy you must embrace if you want to follow Jesus. It means your faith and prayers do not always need to be positive and encouraging. It means you can cry out in the pain, but be determined you will not give up until dawn, trusting God *will* meet you there even though you don't know exactly when. So keep wrestling and hold on until morning, even if "morning" means when He comes back to free us in the ultimate sense.

You recognize how God is referred to throughout Scripture—the God of Abraham, Isaac, and who? Jacob! Think about this for one moment. After the wrestling God changed Jacob's name to Israel. Yet, for the rest of history God wishes to be called the God of *Jacob*. Jacob means "deceiver," and it is a reflection of the worst parts of his life. When asked of God, "Whom shall I say sent me?" God says, "Tell them it is the God of Abraham, Isaac, and Jacob." May it be a bit of encouragement to you that God is the God of your bad times as much as He is of your good times. This God says, "I am here and I am present in your wrestling and struggle. I am here in your pain as much as I am in your joy."

Let us not forget that Jacob walked away with a limp. He asked for a blessing from God, and he got a limp. He found transformation, but he still walked away limping. He began wrestling as an arrogant, insensitive man and came out of it a limping leader who had seen God face to face. What is the purpose of a limp? Why did he have a limp even though he was transformed?

We know his injury was not debilitating because he continued wrestling and even walked away. He was not debilitated, but the limp was a humble reminder of his wrestling match with God. Notice the way Jacob responded to the situation in verse 30 of Genesis 32. Even though he prevailed in the wrestling, he said, "I have seen God face to face, and yet my life has been delivered." He could have looked at his wrestling with God and claimed the victory he had gained. Instead, he was humbly reminded that God could have torn him up but spared him instead. He would have that limp for the remainder of his life to remind him of his struggle with God and the fact that he was able to see God face-to-face and live. Jacob would always have the limp to remind him of the struggle that brought about this transformation.

Our transformation often comes with a struggle, and we walk away with a limp in our heart and spirit as a reminder of a transformation in our lives.

After speaking about the struggle and the wrestling, I once had a man come to me who was an inspector for mixed martial arts. He reminded me that even the ones who win these matches are pretty beat-up. Even the moments we come through victorious are complete with scars and open wounds.

Have you ever played scar wars? We played it in various student leadership circles in my years working in higher education. Taking turn, everyone points to one of their scars and tells the story. Best story wins! Every time we play, we are excited to see if we win.

Bill won the game every time. His story involved a lawn mower accident while wearing flip-flops on a wet slope of grass, if you catch my drift. Bill would always go last, which, in hindsight, was a jerk move. We all told our best stories with all the flare we could muster, but our losing the game was always a foregone conclusion. It would come around to Bill and he would say, "Well! I have three and a half toes." Okay Bill, you win! You always do.

Do you notice how proud we are of our scars? Why are we so proud to win a game like scar wars? Those scars came from painful moments, so why are we so proud of them now? We are proud of the story and are even eager to have the best story, because it means we came *through* great pain. We were tried and not found wanting. We were tested by a great trial, but we came through. That alone makes the pain and scar worth it. The honor in the struggle counterbalances the limp.

We all want change in our lives. We desire transformation. We want God to change our lives, but that can come with a struggle, a story, a wrestling. Transformation is not a switch; it is a process. If we really want our lives to be transformed, it will be a process that often includes difficulty. It will include wrestling.

Understand something—we do not wrestle against God; we wrestle *with* Him. We are constantly fighting against our old nature, and that is why life will always come with a match. We will always walk through life with a limp. That limp is a gift, and we have to understand it as such. We will know many moments of transformation in life, but we should always come out on the other side with a limp. It is a humbling reminder that we have experienced God and yet He has allowed us to go on. It proves we need God to love us. It is our honor to tell the story.

Your limp proves you need God, you have been through great struggles, and you came out closer to the heart of God. It is for this reason you should never trust a Christian who walks without a limp. The true follower of Jesus who has engaged the heart below the machine will be the first to share the vulnerable places of her struggle.

There is victory in the life of the believer, but the victorious life does not always match my day-to-day reality. There is a disservice we find in a presentation of the gospel that promises all things will be rainbows and Bar-B-Que. No, the life of following Jesus does not guarantee constant comfort and fanfare. "Idyllic descriptions of victory in Jesus are more often colored by cultural and personal expectations than by Christ and gospel."[27] There are indeed great stories of people who come to Jesus and gain many honors—but they are not to be expected for every follower of Jesus.

In fact, the gospel as presented in the New Testament portrays a life better categorized as a limp. Jesus is not our victorious King because he never winced, spoken up or questioned, but because having winced, spoken up, and questioned, He remained faithful. Anyone who would come and call himself a follower of Jesus ought to live with the same expectations.

The true disciples of Jesus are not obsessed with getting new revelations, nor are they focused on mastering every chapter and verse of the Bible. What makes a true disciple of Jesus is faithfulness. Pommeled by failure, assaulted by their own breakdowns, and injured by loneliness and mockery, the true disciples may have fumbled and fallen, suffered lapses and relapses, and found themselves among the pigs longing for home. Yet, they kept coming back to the Father.

Those who have revived trust in the heart of the gospel below the machine have come to a better relationship with their past. Your past does serve a purpose, and it is not to be completely forgotten. Your past is a point of reference, not a point of residence. You simply have no time left to be concerned with the past. Allow your past its proper place, but do not give it any more than that. Quit tripping on things that are behind you.

The heart of the gospel below the machine also informs our understanding of acceptance and adequacy. We cannot project onto God our own standards of acceptance. We try so hard on Sundays to make Him love us, rather than living our life as though he already loves us.

When you look at Peter, the rock who sank like a stone too many times, you find the heart of Jesus for the broken ones. Peter built his relationship with Jesus just like a good little machine, made up of his desire for adequacy and acceptance. Is it any wonder he was shattered so greatly when he denied his Lord? His entire machine was dependent on his own muscle, devotion, and accuracy. It was entirely self-generated.

Peter actually believed his relationship with Christ was dependent on his regularity in doing everything right, which would, in his view, earn him approval and acceptance. When Peter's machine inevitably failed, he could only know enormous guilt and shame. He did not catch the heart of Jesus until grace was restored to him after he laid down his arrogant declaration, "Even if I have to die with you, I will never disown you" (Matt. 26:35) for a more healthy realization of his guilt: "Jesus, you *know* I love you" (John 21:17).

Guilt is a reality, but Christians should know the difference between healthy and unhealthy guilt, because there is a difference. The trouble is that many of us will find ourselves in the unhealthy guilt that degrades and denies the grace of Christ in our lives.

Unhealthy guilt wallows. It has a distain for God's gift of real grace. It is entirely preoccupied with the self. It is self-destructive. It is self-demeaning. It is self-defeating. Because of this, unhealthy guilt can lead to a depression and despair. Unhealthy guilt is not concerned with a compassionate God. It uses the harsh and abusive language of rejection and condemnation. Unhealthy guilt easily and quickly becomes larger than life itself.

As the complete opposite, healthy guilt is not naïve or cheap, but it does acknowledge the wrong. Healthy guilt does recognize the depravity and the mistakes. It recognizes these things and feels a true remorse. But healthy guilt does not reside in the past; it only refers to the past. Healthy guilt is able to move forward after remorse, free to embrace the offered gift of forgiveness. Healthy guilt turns its focus toward the realization of forgiveness and redemption instead of the forgotten past.

While we are addressing the difference between healthy and unhealthy guilt, it is important to also highlight the difference between hurt and shame. They should not be wrapped up together, but we often do. Hurt is something done to us. Hurt is inflicted. Hurt and pain are warning systems, and we ought to run to our Abba in those moments. Shame is something we do to ourselves. These are lies about who we really are, and we ought to run to our Abba in those moments as well.

There is an element of the human condition that hates to be powerless in front of others. Studies have shown this regarding the ill. Patients often want so badly not to appear powerless; they have a complete contempt for being ill because of the sense of guilt they feel for having to depend on someone else. They work themselves into an utter delusion in order to avoid this sense of guilt. "All this false guilt about illness is a very common cause of culpable self-neglect."[28] We are so afraid of feeling dependent on someone else that we would actually neglect caring for ourselves in order to avoid it.

One of my resident assistants said once, "I have felt like I have been letting everyone down." I asked him how it was he thought or felt this way. He said he just felt like he was failing in lots of things.

"Maybe I shouldn't be doing this," he said.

"Now *that* would let me down," I said.

I continued to assure him that he had not let me down, and the reason was because I expected him to fail. He would make plenty of mistakes and poor choices as an RA, and I expected him to do so. I told him that by knowing this, he would now be a better RA.

My relationship with Christ soared once I realized God expected me to fail. Why? God's expectation of my failure means he does not expect me to be perfect. Now that is good news! There is freedom in knowing God expects me to fail and loves me despite my mistakes and trips. There is freedom because now I can take more risks. I can go after my faith without abandon or fear. I no longer have to maintain the perfect Christian façade. I can now dive into my faith headfirst.

"But you still make mistakes!"

Yes! I certainly do, and those mistakes will go challenged. Each poor choice, mistake, and failure will come with its fair share of conviction and consequence. There will be mistakes that come along, but God expects those; they do not surprise him, and He loves me despite them.

My RA was able to learn from his failures and face confrontation when it happened, knowing I expected him to fail from time to time. With the assurance that I did not expect him to be perfect, he went all out, taking risks that some of his choices would go wrong, instead of obsessively sidestepping potential failures. He did not have to be perfect or even the best RA. I never expected him to be.

I said to him, "You will not let me down by failing. The only way you will let me down is if you give up."

God expects more failure out of us than we do. We do not let God down when we fail, make mistakes, or ask big questions. We only let God down when we give up simply because we are not willing to fail. Where is the faith, trust, and risk in that?

Paul knew there would be plenty of chances to struggle and potentially fail in a life following Jesus:

> ...though if I should wish to boast, I would not be a fool, for I would be speaking the truth; but I refrain from it, so that no one may think more of me than he sees in me or hears from me. So to keep me from becoming conceited because of the surpassing greatness of revelations, a thorn was given me in the flesh, a messenger of Satan to harass me, to keep me from becoming conceited. Three times I pleaded with the Lord about this, that it should leave me. But he said to me, "My grace is sufficient for you, for my power is made perfect in weakness." (2 Cor. 12:6-9)

What is the thorn? It is much more than you may have pictured. I had always imagined it as the incessant and irritating daily remainder to our soul. You, like me, may have often pictured a glorified splinter that reminds Paul daily that he is to be weak in order for God to bestow His power. But there has to be much more to this thorn.

If it were only a glorified splinter, Paul would be a big baby to plead three times for the Lord to take it away. Come on! Would a big splinter be worthy of such pleading? Suck it up, Paul!

In those times, "thorns" were used as a military device, and it was certainly much more than a splinter. It was more like a big stake in the ground. Soldiers would pound these stakes (not much bigger than a thick tent stake, but sharper and more jagged) into the ground all over the open area they were retreating through. This way, when the enemy came running through that field in pursuit, they would be slowed down. Big stakes protruding from the ground would slow any army down.

Now re-imagine the thorn in the flesh. It takes on a little more intensity. Why would Jesus want Paul to receive a thorn? Paul was an amazing man whose testimony was a rock for the Christian faith. He wrote most of the New Testament. With accomplishments like that, can you imagine the arrogance he would be capable of exerting? But he was not too terribly arrogant. In fact, he was quite humble and vulnerable in his ministry. I think God gave Paul the thorn in order that he might remain humble.

The torment of the thorn brought Paul to this kind of humility that reached millions. This thorn made him *feel* so weak that he could only depend on God. This thorn cut deep into Paul but was never removed. It remained to continually bring Paul to brokenness and vulnerability, but it is this very brokenness that forced Paul to rely so heavily on God. It is a reminder that it is not by our strength, but God's, that we could achieve anything.

In Eugene Peterson's Bible translation, *The Message*, he calls the thorn a "gift of hardship." It really can be anything for us. We do not know exactly what Paul's "thorn" actually was, but we know what it did. Our "thorn" could be anything as long as it does one thing—it ought to bring us to brokenness and vulnerability before a powerful God.

What might your gift of hardship be? What might God have given you? Do you wrestle with addictive behavior that demands you be deliberate every day and attend meetings to keep you from relapse? Do you navigate the broken system to provide love and care to children without it? Are you especially fragile with a tendency to loneliness, worry, depression, or anxiety? Are you a single parent learning how to receive gifts and help from people instead of trying to stand up in all your indestructible power to do it yourself? Do you have wounds from your abusive past that have scarred over years ago? Is it cancer, diabetes, or another terminal disease? Are you tempted every day to resentment, bitterness, pornography, anger, hate, adultery, fantasy?

Do you have too many "gifts of hardship" to count? Are you relentlessly harsh with yourself? Have you ever thought about these gifts that drive you to brokenness? The "gift" is the kicker, isn't it? We certainly get the hardship part of it, but the *gift* is much harder to stomach. I do not mean to imply all hardships are gifts. Some of them are results of sins we have chosen to maintain. Some of them are patterns we allow to continue. Some are imposed upon us. But some may just be gifts that we have prayed relentlessly for God to take away. They may be gifts if you can see how they have driven you to be less arrogant about your accomplishments and more vulnerably accepting of God's power to rescue you again and again.

TELESCOPES TO HEAVEN

PEOPLE LIKE AUGUSTINE and Aquinas argued that God had created the best of all possible worlds, but you would have to be the most optimistic and nearly delusional person in the world to make a statement like that today.

Suffering and pain call our most basic beliefs about God into question. People who probably had not had a passing thought about God for months or years will suddenly lash out at Him in anger when something bad happens to them or someone they love. Much of the question and mental turmoil gets at the issue of cause. If God is truly in control of this planet, then why does He do nothing? Why does he allow it? A lot of it also comes from our understanding of pain in the American culture.

We do everything we can to avoid pain. The painkiller drug business generates nearly 80 billion dollars a year. Studies in London have shown that the British suffer gladly for a cause more commonly than Americans. Indian cultures expect suffering and learn not to fear it. Americans commonly suffer less than anyone else in the world but fear it the most. We are a culture obsessed with not feeling pain, not by acting tough but by trying to be rid of pain. There is a great problem in this.

When you have dental work done on one tooth, you will usually want Novocain. The dentist gives the shot to numb the area around the tooth, but it is never just the one tooth, is it? That tooth and the surrounding area are often numbed with one pinpointed shot. This is the way Novocain works.

In the same way, when something happens to cause us emotional pain, we do what we can to get rid of the pain, such as by numbing it with whatever we can. For some, it may be with drugs and alcohol. For others it is relationships or sex. But like Novocain, it is never just the pain that gets numbed. Once you go numb to pain, you go numb to many other feelings.

Dr. Paul Brand[29] works at a leprosarium in India and has written stories about patients there who, after accidentally dropping something in a fire, will reach into the fire to grab it. With a painless, straight face, they recover the object with a melted hand. Without pain, they never realize there is a problem.

We think leprosy is a disease where your skin falls off and you lose your limbs, but that is not really the disease of leprosy. The real disease of leprosy is the loss of the functions of the nerve endings. The means the patient cannot feel pain. When you cannot feel pain, you may not realize you have been burned, struck, or cut. So the wound or injury goes unattended, because you do not feel or realize it. Then it gets infected and maybe a limb or two are forever lost. Essentially, a leper is one who cannot feel pain, a condition that leaves his wounds untended and infected.

Do you see the weight of this? Inability to feel pain is not a super power; it is a disease!

In my numbness to painful situations in my life, I

have left my wounded heart untended. I have numbed to a point where I do not realize there is a problem. I just want the pain to go away. So I numb the pain while the wound remains. I am a leper!

Pain is a gift. Our conscience is a gift to alert us to spiritual and emotional harm. But we often allow our consciences to be seared like an iron (1 Tim. 4:2), and we no longer feel anything.

We are wounded people; that is a fact. Pain is unpleasant by definition and by effectiveness, but it is that very quality that saves us from destruction. Pain is a communication network and should be viewed as such. Pain sends a message to the person who is suffering: "Attend to me! I need help!"

Many Christians who believe in a loving God and Creator do not know how to interpret pain. We have a sense that we think the world is meant to be comfortable, so when suffering happens, it complicates our worldview. In a drastically hurting world where the most common question asked of God is, "Why is there pain?" we need to learn how to engage that question.

Even though pain may have been intended as a warning system, something on this planet has gone erratically wrong and pain is raging out of control. Now there exists more than just pain, it now includes suffering. There now exists a deep human misery. God has set into motion certain natural laws that can be perverted and misguided by our freedom to choose what we do with those things, and much has been perverted. Even what was intended to be a protective warning system—pain—is subject to the same abuse as every other gift God has given to us.

Because of the freedom we have, human beings

introduced something new to the planet—rebellion against God's original plan. The Bible traces the entrance of suffering and evil into the world to our human choices. *Homo sapiens* is the only species released from the restriction of instinct. We actually have a choice. Chesterton said we are the only wild animal.

Theologians like to attribute all of the world's pain and suffering to Genesis 3 and the fall. Paul elaborates on it some more in Romans 8. Pain and suffering multiplied on earth as a consequence of the abuse of our freedom. Since the fall, we have been emitting a constant stream of spoil to the point that we now live on what Paul calls "a groaning planet." (Rom. 8:22)

There is a common myth that has driven the question of pain that we have all been asking for centuries. The myth is that God is a cruel and unloving God. It is as if God is somehow aloof from our groaning and our pain and our suffering. Has it ever seemed in your pain as though God was nowhere to be found?

> When the Bridegroom leaves, the bride feels forsaken. Medieval writers call this the 'wound of love'. She is wounded, or 'smitten,' in that she is dramatically in love with him and cannot bear to live without him.[30]

The reality of our pain and struggle comes from a wound that goes deeper than our own individual hurts and hang-ups. All of our hurt and struggle is rooted in the pain of our lost connection with our Great Love.

If we accept the fact that suffering is part of this life, whether we like it or not, we have to discover how to see Jesus and get through suffering. How are we to engage the heart and remain faithful through our suffering? It will require a great amount of resilience, but resilience will bring us where God intended us to be.

If you look at a hurricane, you will see all the destruction it causes in its wake. But meteorologists say if you can look at the center in the eye of the storm, you will notice a tranquil peace. When we are faced with suffering and hurt, we can feel as though our lives are raging and being torn apart by the storm. But that's not the complete picture. There is comfort to be found in the fact that "God is our refuge and strength; a very present help in trouble" (Ps. 46:1). God is a refuge and a hiding place. Sometimes in the midst of suffering we just need refuge. We need a hiding place where Jesus can comfort us. Sometimes when life vibrates out of our control, we just need to hold on to something constant and rooted.

Even Jesus needed a hiding place. He was often found wandering away to be alone, but He was never actually alone. Jesus found his hiding place in the heart of His Father.

Jesus is present in our suffering. This is why I love Psalm 46:1. It does not say, "God will take all your trouble away." It says He is present in your trouble. He may not say a word, but there is a hiding place in His heart. There is comfort found in the same Jesus who, though he fully intended to raise Lazarus from the dead, still stopped to weep with the hurting family. He did not cry a little; he wept. His gut was wrenched. He was going to raise Lazarus from the dead, but he still took the time to weep for his friend.

In times of your greatest suffering and hurt, who have been the most comforting people? Has it been the ones who have timid clichés learned from the greeting cards at the grocery store?

"It is going to be okay."

"God has brought this about for a reason."

"God has a plan."

"Here is a casserole!"

Or has it been those who have sat with you while you ached? Have the most comforting person been the one who did all she could to enter into your pain? Jesus is a present help in the trouble. Do you know this is true? I do not mean to ask if this is correct or the right answer, but to you, is this true?

Once you come to know Jesus who is present in your pain, you have truly taken hold of the heart below the machine. The truly broken and hurting have the greatest capacity to engage the heart of Jesus. David Gibbons attaches the brokenhearted to those who live on the fringes:

> If the pain does not first kill or numb them, people on the fringe experience the flow of a supernatural God because they are broken open.... They often experience a supernatural transformation of their pain into a power to relieve the suffering of others.[31]

Suffering and pain have an enormous capacity for shaping your life. It goes beyond Paul's thorn and keeps us from focusing entirely on our gifts, talents, and higher qualities. Pain can become a blessing in life because it points to your destiny, gives credibility to your voice, connects you to other people, provides fellowship that binds you to others, and breaks you open for living water.[32]

Can you see how to engage the beating heart under the beaten machine of pain? I once heard it said, but I do not recall who said it: "The Church is like a battered woman. The more bruises she has, the more makeup she puts on." This is very common with those who are abused. In an attempt to protect the abuser, but more detrimentally, in an attempt to hide their own obvious need for help, battered women will put on a lot of makeup to cover the scars and bruises.

Eventually battered women start to look fake with all of the makeup. As they layer on the multicolored products on their faces, nobody realizes anything is actually wrong. Why does nobody care about this woman who is abused and battered? Because nobody realizes that she is being abused. Nobody can see the dire need for love, care, or protection. She becomes fragile but artificial. Nobody takes the time to care for her. She covers her pain, but more dangerously, she covers her need.

The litany of pain that accompanies abuse affects your entire life. Wounds to your heart and soul take longer to heal than physical wounds and are even more hidden. They are personal and private. This is why people feel isolated, misunderstood, unapproved, and alone because they are afraid to remove the mask and let people see the real pain of being violated, abandoned, or discarded.

The Father's children have become battered and bruised, but they have covered up their hurt, pain, and reality with spiritual cosmetics. We all have wounds and pain, but we cover them up and keep anyone and everyone from seeing what really lies beneath. In so doing, we have come to appear frighteningly counterfeit and artificial. We become people who nobody wants to approach, because we are simply unreal. We are artificial, have-it-all-together, tattered men and women who deflect people who could help us heal the wounds.

We have neutered the gospel when we mask ourselves with spiritual cosmetics. We become a sect of people who deny our pain and wounds, and in so doing become people nobody can, nor wants to, relate to. Humans know pain and relate to those who can come alongside one another to heal. When we cover up our pain and our wounds, we appear naïve, and Christians are often the worst. People have no desire to relate to anyone who is naïve about pain.

The heart of the gospel that beats beneath your machine is one of a God who hurts when you hurt and weeps over your wounds. You verbally claim a belief in gospel about a God who created a people who would operate as a body. When a part of the body is wounded and exposed, the body begins to heal. That is the body we were created to be, the body the gospel rings of, but we neuter the gospel when we cover our wounds. We cover it up with spiritual makeup and keep anyone from seeing that the pain is real. When we hide our wound, we hide a gospel we claim to believe in. We hide a God we claim to believe in. We also hide the gospel and God not only from ourselves, but also from the needy around us. Healing only happens with each wound revealed.

We are all wounded people, and all those wounds left alone to infection will hinder our ability to know God more intimately. They hinder our ability to relate well. For this reason, it is with each wound healed that the voice of God grows that much clearer. That is my ultimate goal—for the voice of God to grow clearer and clearer each day. I hear God's voice in my soul more clearly than I did a year ago, a month ago, or even compared to yesterday because I have gone into myself with God's guidance and unchangeable light. It is not easy and is often met with some fear and hurt, but the unchangeable light goes with me into the darkened and forgotten recesses of my inner self to shed some of that light upon the wounds that have affected my ability to hear the voice of God more clearly and more intimately.

Intimacy has often been defined in Christian church-talk as "into me see." Denying intimacy to the ones you love the most is hiding what is really inside you. You are not willing to let them see who you really are, and you make all attempts to hide. This is not only applicable to marriages, but to God as well. Though He already knows all that is within me, how much am I willing to reveal to Him? That determines my desire for actual intimacy.

A majority of us can admit to a need for change within ourselves. We know the parts of our lives where change is needed. For some of us, we know these things well as we continually obsess over them and dwell on them for long periods of time. A majority of us, if asked, could give a great account of the deep wounds and hurts as well as the hang-ups and struggles that plague us. We know where change is needed. We know where healing is needed in our lives.

When I began working in recovery and crisis ministry, I received some initial training in several recovery programs and processes. The training required that I engage myself in the process and the environment. It required me to actually look at myself, self-evaluate, and wrestle with the issues that arose. I dealt with the wounds I had hidden. I dealt with some addictive behaviors, coping tendencies, and past hurt. I was trained in this fashion in order to truly walk with the guests in the ministry who are on their road to recovery and healing.

What great relief we would know if we could be healed! How wonderful it would be if there was a great healer and physician to heal and bring change to the areas we most need them!

Some of us would say, "But there is!" There is a great physician who is capable of changing and healing those areas that darken our daily lives. We know God calls us to Him for that healing and change.

There is one problem! We typically come to God without those things that need to be healed and changed. We come to God with our churchy selves, fluffy words, fake actions, and spiritual presentations. We come with all the pretty parts and leave the ugly parts that need the healing and change.

We "come to God" in our prayer, but how do we pray? What do we pray? Do we come praying all of the pretty words we have learned? Do we pray the pretty things that look spiritual?

What a shame that we who know we need healing refuse to bring the parts of ourselves that need change before the master healer and physician! Transformation and change is possible for us who need it so desperately, yet we refuse to bring those areas before God who is capable and willing to heal and transform.

One of the things that keeps us from being closer to the heart of God or from healing is control. We are always running after and holding on to control. We want to control everything and everyone. Then when we realize we cannot, it is devastating to our personal world. It is for this reason we do not really want to be broken. It is for this reason we are unable to really be what God wants us to be: whole. It is for this reason we feel like our lives are actually "out of control." It is a great irony.

In Scripture, God is continually calling us into the desert place. There is healing in the desert if we would only go. But the desert is terrifying. Some part of us knows if we go into the desert, we will be forced to journey, and on a wilderness journey you do not control what happens. "People will ultimately come to terms with God, with destiny, and with themselves only when they dare to seek aloneness."[33] You are alone, and that means you are your own company. Most of us could think of no worse company because when we are alone we have nobody to impress or control. We have to look at ourselves and deal with things we typically avoid by directing our attention and focusing on other people.

The desert has healing and peace that await us, but we do not really want it because it requires that we relent our control.

The hurt, the pain, the addictive behaviors, the selfishness, the anger, the bitterness, the fear, the jealousy are all within us, and in order to not feel or deal with those things, we react with control. As long as we can control our world around us, we will never have to look at or reveal those wounds within.

Real healing and peace will happen when we give up thinking we can control things and people, and begin to live a life of trust and healing. An incredible experience of Jesus lies just beyond that decision to lay down our control and see what Jesus is about to do. Martha learned this lesson in one of the best encounters with Jesus in all of history.

Do you remember when Martha's brother, Jesus' close friend, Lazarus was deathly ill? Both of his sisters send word to Jesus: "Lord, he whom you love is ill" (John 11). Jesus decided not to go to Lazarus immediately. These were very close friends of Jesus. He loved this family (vs. 5), but he decided to stay with his disciples for two more days. Jesus told them they were going to go to Lazarus once he had died. By the time Jesus arrived, Lazarus had already been in the tomb for four days. He was as dead as one can get.

Martha heard that Jesus was coming to them, and she stormed out to meet him on the road (vs. 20). Her indignant response set the stage for the rich interaction. She came stomping up to him and said, "Lord, if you had been here, my brother would not have died." Have you ever had even one indignant moment in your mind and heart toward Jesus? Have you ever wanted to scream out, "Jesus, if you had just been there?" Of course you have. Here is what makes this so nuts: Martha was right!

I imagine Jesus could have answered her immediately, "I know, Martha. If I had come when you wanted me to, in the way you wanted, Lazarus would not have died. But if I had come when you wanted me to, in the way you wanted, you would not have been able to encounter me in the way you are about to in a few minutes."

You see, Martha knew Jesus could heal. She had watched him do it. Her experience of Jesus as a healer was already established. But she had never encountered Jesus as one who could raise someone from the dead. If Jesus had showed up at the moment Martha sent word, He could have healed Lazarus, but she would never have had the same encounter with Jesus that she did when Lazarus was brought back from the tomb alive.

She knew Jesus would heal him. It is as though he was saying, "You would not have come to know me more and deeper than you are about to know me. You would not have been prepared for an even greater revelation of me than you had already known."

God's silence in your life means He is prepared to bring into your life an even greater revelation of Himself than you have ever known. When God is silent, start watching for what He is about to teach you about Himself. This will require faith, trust, and anticipation.

One of the most familiar passages of Scripture is Psalm 23, especially if you have ever been to a funeral or memorial. The last verse says, "Surely goodness and mercy shall follow me all the days of my life." Have you, like me, always missed the most important word in that phrase: *follow*?

One of the unchanging attributes of God is His goodness. God is always good, and He is always in control of our lives and world. But we still face difficult and painful things in life. We still have trouble. We still have hurt and horrible circumstances we go through and come through. Where is the goodness in those moments?

One of the most often quoted passages, Psalm 23, reveals that goodness in the most painful moments of life is just behind you. It follows you all the days of your life. God's goodness is coming. God's love and kindness is coming. It is always behind you.

We are never promised that all things that happen in life are good. We are promised, however, that no matter what happens, goodness will follow. In all things, goodness will follow. It is always behind you, and it is coming.

DEEPER SENSES OF HOME

WHEN I SEARCH my heart and find my faith lacking, it is less about doubt than it is about fear. My lacking faith is really my increasing fear. I fear a great many things, and I wonder how or if certain things will happen. I am afraid of certain outcomes happening and other outcomes not happening. I am confident in who God is and what He is able to do. So my lacking faith is not so much about the doubts I have but about my fears and worries at particular points in life.

The beautiful machines of faith we have built allow us to profess our faith in God's unconditional love while being haunted by a great many fears. Look at the many "if" questions reeling in our minds.

> What am I going to do if I do not find a spouse, a house, a job, a friend, a benefactor? What am I going to do if they fire me, if I get sick, if an accident happens, if I lose my friends, if my marriage does not work out, if war breaks out? What if tomorrow the weather is bad, the buses are on strike, or an earthquake happens? What if someone steals my money, breaks into my house, rapes my daughter, or kills me?[34]

It comes to a point when these types of questions guide our day-to-day lives, and we start to get harassing phone calls from the creditors of fear and worry.

Many Christians seek a God who is far too small because they can manage a small God according to their own standards. The trouble with this is that when their god is too small, the only way they can respond to the world and the circumstances around them is with fear, anxiety, hopelessness, and helplessness. This is their only option because their god truly is not big enough. Their god cannot do anything for them in these experiences. They may say with their mouth and mind that he can, but their heart and perceptions do not really believe it. Their fear reveals how small their god actually is.

You cannot be blamed entirely for the fear that runs your life. Our culture is more and more designed to keep you fearful. Our media is full of fearmongers who profit a great deal by keeping you terrified. The goal is to have you submit to their control. "In exchange for your submission, Fearmongers offer strength and protection, which, for many, is a security they are willing to trade their freedom for."[35] The fearmongers commonly have a devoted team of fearful, submissive personalities and viewers at their beckoning.

We are designed to worship, and we will either worship God or something else. You can determine what that is by looking at your time and passions. We might be sobered to compare the time we spend at worship with the time spent working ourselves into a frenzy by watching round-the-clock news channels. "It is difficult to claim that God is our ultimate concern, the center of our being, when politics claims so much of our time and our emotions."[36] We might be greatly surprised if we could be greatly honest in this reflection.

You would be surprised with how easy it is to convince American people that a man is a demon to be feared. In his book *Scary Close*, Donald Miller speaks of a gathering he attended on Capitol Hill where he struck up a conversation with a political strategist. It is this man's job to attack opposing candidates. Miller remembers the man to be truly sweet and tender, but he said, "It is my job to scare senior citizens in southern Florida and convince them their medical benefits are going to be taken away." After this conversation, Miller reflected, "all the clanging pots and pans in the kitchen to scare people from the territory we feel compelled to defend is playing into the hands of dark forces."[37]

Something has me greatly concerned as we look at the world around us today. You may be thinking, "Oh really, just one thing?" It is not hard to be discouraged by the things we see, is it? You do not have to look much further than the evening news to realize things are terribly broken in our world today, but these are not the things that concern me today.

There is injustice and a lack of peace in our world. There is a dramatic lack of truth and morality in our culture. There is an evil that pervades most of the arenas we live in today. But still none of these is my biggest concern. What concerns me more than any of these things is the perspective and worldview of most Christians. My friends, it would seem most Christians today live their lives in response to the enemy instead of in response to the hope, faith, and promise of Jesus Christ. It would seem many Christians choose to live in fear of the world around them instead of in confident expectation of the promises of the Christ they say they trust.

Far too many have come to believe and accept their tickets to ride on a certain hand basket set for a certain destination. Something is terribly wrong. "A fatalistic worldview is cancer of the spirit."[38] Paul writes to Timothy and speaks about false teachers and prophets as "those who do not agree with the sound words of our Lord Jesus Christ and teaching that accords with godliness" (1 Tim. 4:3). It is important to remember he is speaking about false teachers and prophets in this context, but put this description up against what you see among Christians today. Put it up against the representation of Christians on your social media feeds.

How often have you found yourself in what Paul goes on to call "unhealthy craving for controversy and for quarrels about words" (vs. 4)? How often have you recognized the news you watch and read producing "envy, dissention, slander, evil suspicions and constant friction" (vv. 4–5)?

But let yourself jump to verse 11 to see how we ought to be living in a culture such as ours. "But as for you, O man of God, flee these things. Pursue righteousness, godliness, faith, love, steadfastness, gentleness." The key word is *pursue*. This is an active word. It *does* something. This word is not content to sit and lob word grenades at the culture. This word is a command to do something.

In Ephesians 4:1, Paul "urges you to walk in a manner worthy of the calling to which you have been called" and that would necessarily make an impact. Impact is a strange thing in the days of social media. There used to be a time when if you wanted to make an impact, you had to show up and do something. You could not simply post or share or like something on the internet and call it activism. The call on the life of a Christian is a strong one, and the heart that beats beneath is going to require that we really show up. If we are to move forward in the call on our lives, we have to be willing to lean into it.

We are to actively pursue a list of things: righteousness, godliness, faith, love, steadfastness, and gentleness. Imagine for a moment if Christians were more concerned with pursuing these things in their own lives instead of the arguments and quarrels they have with the culture around them. We are to "fight the good fight of faith" (vs 12), but it may not be the fight you think. It is not your job to be a warrior against the culture. You are to fight the fight of faith. What does it look like? The answer immediately follows in the next verse. You do so by taking hold of the eternal life to which you were called.

Believers who encounter the heart that beats beneath the machines ought to know the hope that is within them. They must first know what hope is before they can know what to search for within themselves.

The basic meaning of the word for hope in Scripture is "to anticipate." There is a sense of confident expectation. It is not the ethereal well-wishing we have come to understand of hope. To have and possess hope is to have a confident expectation. To hope is to expect and anticipate with an assurance.

Hope is not an attitude we have. There is something to which we direct our life or it's not hope. If hope is a confident expectation, it is natural to wonder: for what are we expecting? What is the hope fixed on? This is the key question for the encounter with hope in Scripture. It is not as elusive as it may seem.

Hope has substance and a strong definition, particularly for the heart beneath the machines. We have every reason to live with hope. Hope is what allows us to have confidence now with an expectation for later. Any sense of hopelessness can likely be traced back to a faulty subject on whom we placed our hope in the first place. Only God is worthy of our utter hope. Only God is worthy of a confident expectation through Christ for salvation and for unconditional certainty for His promises for our future. If I place my hope in anything else, my heart will be crushed.

Yes, the times are changing at the pace of the explosion of internet, and our culture and society are increasingly opposed to the lifestyle of a follower of Jesus, but I see great hope for what will develop by necessity because of these changing times.

First, this is nothing new. God's people have always had to live among a dominant culture that does not affirm their values, lifestyle, or claim to Truth. It may feel new to us who have been believers through a more comfortable time, but we cannot disregard the reality John reminds us of: "this world and its desires are passing away" (1 John 2:17). We will not and cannot turn the world around, and we cannot pretend this opposition is anything new. We stand on the shoulders of believers who have seen exponentially worse realities than anyone who reads this ever will.

Secondly, do not entirely believe the statistics that portray a declining church in America. Understand that correct statistics misinterpreted are false statistics. The Church is still and will continue to be quite great. The question will be whether or not its impact will be strong in the coming generations.

Next, do not disregard your call to discomfort. As circumstances grow less comfortable for the follower of Jesus, it becomes more impossible for the Christian to simply float in and out and up and down on the waves of culture like a pool raft on Malibu Bay. The tide is changing so rapidly that the future generations will be stronger believers because they will simply have to be. Christians will be increasingly marginalized in our culture, but that means the true believers will be exactly that, *true*, valiant believers. The days of lukewarm, mechanical, Jesus-following are swiftly drawing to a close. That is good news!

Lastly, the "God-card" still applies! We must always trust in a sovereign God over and above whatever happens in our culture and world. We ought to hold on forever to the hope of 1 Corinthians 2:9–10: "No eye has seen, no ear has heard, no mind has conceived what God has prepared for those who love Him—but God has revealed it to us by His Spirit."

The opposite of love is not hate; it is fear, and love drives out fear. As we look to the future, we have no reason to fear if we have truly had an experience of the loving God who will remain sovereign, regardless of the paranoia you hear on television or internet. The opposition to love is what astonished Paul in Galatians 1: "I am astonished that you are so quickly deserting him who called you in the grace of Christ and are turning to a different gospel—not that there is another one, but there are some who trouble you and want to distort the gospel of Christ." We have come to listen to the new gospel of fear instead of the gospel of Jesus Christ, which declares hope.

Walter Burghardt wrote, "Life is discouraging, yes;

but remember your hope lies not in constant man and woman but in God, a Yahweh forever faithful. So confess your sins and proceed with confidence to the task at hand. A glorious future beckons."[39] Let us fall back from the fight we lost a long time ago and start to rest upon the hope and confidence found in the One who is forever faithful. Let us turn our attention more often to our personal sins than to the sins of the land. Let us remember our personal task to place more faith in the Lord than in the enemy's current destruction.

This is not a call to stick your hand in the sand, but it is a call to hold your head high. It is not a call to retreat into your own separate bunker, but it is a call to lean into the heartbeat of the Father within you to deal with your sin and walk with Jesus.

"For God has given us a Spirit not of fear but of power and love and self-control" (2 Tim. 1:7). Here is a verse so many Christians love to misuse for the courage to face daunting moments in life. We are reminded in quoting this verse that we ought to not be fearful because God has placed power within us. We quote this verse and challenge one another to live in the power God has given to us instead of neglecting it by living in fear. But there is a misuse here, and it is entirely grammatical.

We are placing a period where there are commas. We read and quote this passage as though all we need to do is not be afraid, but be powerful—period. We have removed the commas and cut off the rest of the passage.

No, you are not given a spirit of fear. Yes, you have been given a spirit of power, *comma*, and love, *comma*, and self-control (discipline). In the most disheartening moments, you are given a spirit of power, love, and discipline. In the most difficult and fearful moments of life, how often have you been challenged to draw upon love and discipline as much as power? Could the spirit of power only be found in the compound of love and discipline? In the daunting moments of life when you are tempted to fear, will you discipline yourself to love God and people, because there is power in that?

Our worry and fear reveal how little we trust God. "No less hurtful is the spirit of fear and distrust in spiritual things, it never really hears what God has to say."[40] There is an unrest that agitates our heart when we seek in our own way and in our own strength the spiritual approval that comes only from Abba. The heart occupied with its own plans and efforts will fail continually at getting the true rest and blessing of Jesus.

In 2013 I spoke for a chapel convocation at a university in southern California, and I was the last speaker for the year. The theme verse for the entire year on which every speaker was to speak was Philippians 4:7, "And the peace of God, which surpasses all understanding, will guard your hearts and your minds in Christ Jesus." I had spent several weeks before giving the message watching videos of previous speakers, in preparation and hopes I did not repeat the same reflections.

I began my message by mentioning that all speakers had been talking about and searching for this peace, which, first of all, is beyond our understanding. The students and speakers had been searching and thinking about it for an entire year. We all want this sort of peace in our lives, but why have we not found it in an entire year of focused search through this verse? I believe most of us fail to find this great peace in verse 7 because we have not read and focused on verse 6.

If this peace is the peace of God, and God is truly

over all, in all, and through all (Eph. 4:6), then this means that peace is available to us right now. This peace we are in a constant search for is here and available now.

Just before the *and* in verse 7, Paul writes, "Do not be anxious about anything, but in everything by prayer and supplication with thanksgiving let your requests be made known to God...." Be anxious in nothing, and pray in everything, *and* the peace of God, which surpasses all your understanding, will guide your heart and mind. The reason we do not have this peace in our lives is because we are praying in nothing, and we are anxious in everything.

Here is the reality: your life is out of control. Allow me to rephrase that: your life is out of your control. We just do not get to control life. If I controlled life, I would be a best friend with Chris Farley, I would play football for the Chicago Bears, and Chicago deep-dish pizza would not make me fat. I do not get to control life.

But we try to control all elements of our life. We try to control our own bodies. As I worked with college students for most of my adult life, I kept watching their eating and living habits, thinking, "I am so jealous, but I also know your body is going to catch up to you." If we could control what happens to our bodies, things like cancer would not happen. We do not get to control life.

We try to control our family and relationships. I wish I could make my family respond to me the way I wanted and do the things I wish they would do. If I could control my family, the things they do that frustrate me would never happen. We simply do not get to control life.

The problem arises again when we keep focusing on all those things we do not get to control. We focus on these things instead of the God of peace, and we begin to get anxious in everything. Anxiety and worry come from those places we try to control that we simply do not get to control.

You will not find peace by just trying to change your environment. We like to think to ourselves, "If I could just change this person or if I could just change this situation, I would finally have some peace." You may be able to influence your environment, but you will never be able to completely change it to be as you wish it to be.

There are moments you want to tell God to pay attention to you. God, listen to me. I am restless in my complaints, and I am moaning for you to hear me (Ps. 55:1-3). When you walk through those times of life, it is okay to have those sorts of emotions. It is okay to voice your complaints, because life will always be at least a little bit crazy. There will always be some chaos stirring around you.

There are times you continue with David in Psalm 55, "Oh that I had wings like a dove! I would fly away and be at rest" (vs 6). You would want to just get away from the chaos you cannot control. But those are the moments you need the most honest prayer your heart can give, and you need to hold verse 16 to heart, "But as for me, I call to God and he will save me." God speaks to you in your chaos and says to you, "If you will get to me, cast all your cares on to me, I will sustain you through it" (v. 22).

We are given the example of prayer in asking God to "give ear to my words; consider my groaning" (Ps. 5:1). Other translations say, "Consider my sighing." Do you realize God knows all the emotions, joy, sorrow, anger, and discouragement that are wrapped up in your groans and sighs? Do you realize God knows all that is behind your guttural moans when you have no words to utter?

The moments you do not even have the words for what you feel and want to express to God, He still knows what all of that means, and He says, "If you will still bring me your truest self, I will hold you."

With what sort of dedication and devotion do you pray in everything? This peace we all crave in the midst of chaos is only going to be found when we come with the desire to engage our heart in prayer, but that prayer cannot be formulated in such a way that it is as heartless as a machine. If you are running your prayer life like a treadmill of activity, you are still not getting anywhere. You will only find the peace that is of God when you are more entangled with Him.

In the triumphal entry, all the people came and laid palm branches before Jesus while crying out, *Hosanna*, which means "rescue me." They were crying out for rescue to the conquering king they had expected for generations. They were pleading for the king who would come and rescue them from all the chaos and oppression over them where they had no control. They had no say in their government; everything was forced upon them. So they screamed out, "Hosanna!"

Even while they begged for rescue, Jesus looked at them he wept for them. The conquering king looks at his people and weeps. Then he said, "If you only knew what would bring you peace—but now it is hidden from your eyes." If you only knew the peace that was available to you! But you are missing it! Over and over again I sit with people who crave a peace beyond their understanding in the lives of chaos, and I cannot help but think, "If you only knew the peace that is available to your heart and life! If you would only pray in everything, and be anxious in nothing."

Prayer is not a magic wand for peace. Prayer is a discipline that lowers anxiety. It lowers the focus on the things of chaos, pain, and the uncontrollable, because when you are praying, you are focused on the God of peace instead of all the things you cannot control. Prayer is taking hold of the Unshakeable One though your life vibrates out of control. Take hold of something solid in your out-of-control life, and Jesus says in John 14, "Peace I leave with you. Peace I give to you. Not as the world gives do I give to you. Let not your hearts be troubled, neither let them be afraid."

Over and over we hear our culture, our country, and our world thrown into that hand basket on a journey to a particular destination. We are caught in this crazy battle to see *how* we ought to be engaged with the culture or whether we even *should* be engaged. We watch different all-day news outlets to solidify our paranoia and anger. We lash out against a culture that left us years ago. We are concerned that this culture is sinking and sinking fast.

What strikes me about realizing we are sinking is too many people are content to shoot holes in a sinking ship—the ship that we all are in.

We drastically misunderstand what it means to be in the world but not of it when we think we can actually escape the world, much less when we attack and shoot holes in it. At some point, it may be helpful to place ourselves specifically into that metaphor. If I were in a sinking boat, regardless of how disgusting that boat may be, I am not going to be content firing holes to expedite the process of sinking. I may even try to do what I can to redeem, repair, and restore as many of the cracks that I can.

What if we were hopeful and lived differently? "Grace

is for the humble, not for the self-satisfied. So a setback, a serious check, the crumbling of a whole majestic world, may be the necessary road to a renaissance. For each of us, a setback can become the opportunity of a return to oneself and a personal meeting with God."[41] What if the decaying realities of our broken and bedraggled culture were challenges to discover potential restoration? If we are unable to see restoration possibilities, we do not understand the gospel at a heart level beneath our own machinery. There ought to be a change in our perspective of crumbling realities around us. Every broken piece is a personal interaction with God waiting to happen.

Do you suppose God expected you to live life without hope? Hope is not a promise of riches and wealth, but God "did expect that life would be human enough so that every child could grow up to think about him and love him.... He did expect the hopeful to lend hope to the hopeless."[42] Every person who has engaged the beating heart of Jesus below their own hopeless machines is a leader with a responsibility to lend what they have to those who lack it. You have every reason to hope, and your responsibility is to look at a hopeless person and give to them what you have. This is how the effect of hope will transfer to those around you if you really believe the hope you have as a lover of Jesus.

Think of a posture of restoration. What would it look like in some of the darkest and most hopeless places? "When we smile, it's a sign of confidence, because fear and paranoia are signaled by frowns, not smiles."[43] Think of the presentation of most Christians today. Look at the realities and connections that business magazines and top leaders have come to realize. I want to look many Christians in the eyes and say, "If you really do have the hope you profess, notify your faces. Notify your posture. Notify your actions." If we believe the gospel with any level of confidence, our attitude ought to be very different.

If you saw me, your first inclination is very unlikely to be, "I bet he is a lifeguard." You would be correct, but I have seen *Baywatch* (Millennials: *Baywatch* is a show from the 1900s about California lifeguards). My wife also used to be a lifeguard, and she has explained to me some of the primary points of an open-water rescue. It is dangerous for the lifeguard to approach a flailing adult because it puts the lifeguard in danger as well. The lifeguard would swim out to the drowning victim who is in over their head and yell out for the person to stop flailing so that he may be approached for rescue.

Can you hear the voice of Jesus talking to you when you are in over your head? He says to you, "Stop flailing! I am here to rescue you. Peace is available to you. It was always available to you.

WHEN THE MIGHTY DESCEND AND THE LOWLY RISE

THERE WAS A moment you can likely remember if you sit still long enough. Can you remember when you had a real encounter with something greater than you? Many of you will know this as a time you encountered Jesus Christ. It was time you were ambushed by joy, peace, confidence, and love. You allowed for enough awe and wonder to be deeply moved and entangled with the heart of Jesus.

But over time, you took on the demands of life and ministry. You got distracted and distant from that beautiful moment. You started to treat Jesus like that high school friend who is now your online friend. You check in when your social media reminds you it is his birthday. You may peruse his wall once in a while, but you know you have entirely lost track of the friendship. It never crosses your mind to meet with him, and something else always comes up even if you tried. You remember your love very fondly, but the memory fades with each day.

You have allowed your relationship with Jesus to fade into agnosticism. Agnosticism is chosen inattention. It is a lack of discipline and dedication to the relationship, and His presence grows more and more inaccessible. We have ignored the relationship long enough that it has been choked out. It isn't that you deny God as a personal Father; it is that you have ignored the love affair long enough that it has grown unimaginable. I keep saying "you," but I know far too well how to describe this distance. It is far too familiar.

My meager attempts at prayer are filled with unnatural phrases addressed to an emotionless god, and I realize in those moments I have abandoned real prayer. I have allowed my faith to settle into good little acts of charity and fluffy phrases I have learned over decades of churchgoing. On the days when God's love ambushes me and I come back to him, a part of me expects God to say, "Who in the world are you?"

None of my failed faithfulness has proven lethal yet. Over and over, grace is lavished on me in the very core of my heart and soul. God's forgiveness has been given to me in outlandish pours. I came groveling back to my Father, and He saw me from a long way off. He took pity on me and ran to me. Do you know how ridiculous it is to know God came running for you?

Every time I come pleading for God to give me the forgiveness He already gave, I hear Him speak to my heart: "Has it ever occurred to you that I am already greatly proud of you? Has it crossed your guilt-ridden mind that I have loved your willingness to choose me after I chose you? Have you, for even one moment, thought I love the fact that you did not give up entirely, but you came to me again and again?" Nearly every prayer I lob from my weakly faith returns to me with this interaction.

How do we come to know God so intimately to hear

Him speak these things to our heart? How do we grow closer to Him? How do we come to a point where we can say our relationship with God is going well?

Psalm 42:7 says, "Deep calls to deep at the roar of your waterfalls; all your breakers and your waves have gone over me." Perhaps somewhere in the depths of your life you have heard that call to something deeper and fuller. You have become weary of shallow experiences and typical life and faith. That is really the great search every one of us is obsessed with discovering. Our culture is cursed by superficial and instant satisfaction, and the need for God goes far deeper than that. The need and search for God goes into the inner life.

The disciplines of the inner life, if you dedicated yourself to them, can lead you to a richer and fuller inner life where God desires to meet you. But there is a requirement for you before you even begin. You have one task! The primary requirement is a longing after God.

> As a deer pants for flowing streams, so pants my soul for you, O God. My soul thirsts for God, for the living God. When shall I come and appear before God? (Psalm 42:1–2)

The change we need inside us in order to come closer to the heart of God is one only God can bring about. That being said, do not allow yourself to float to the other side of things and begin thinking, "Well, I guess there is nothing I can do."

You cannot make yourself holy; only God can change you. But spiritual disciplines allow you to place yourself before God so that He can transform you. Galatians 6:8 says, "For the one who sows to his own flesh will from the flesh reap corruption, but the one who sows to the Spirit will from the Spirit reap eternal life." Think of it this way: a farmer does not grow anything. All he can do is make the conditions right for growth. He cultivates and works the soil. He plants seed, waters, fertilizes. But at some point the earth takes over and up comes the growth.

This is how disciplines work. They put us where God can work change in our lives. The disciplines *do* nothing. They do not save you. They do not change you. Only God changes your heart, but the disciplines are how we put ourselves in a place where God can do amazing things of change in our lives. Jesus said:

> If you ask me anything in my name, I will do it. If you love me, you will keep my commandments. And I will ask the Father, and he will give you another Helper, to be with you forever, even the Spirit of truth, whom the world cannot receive, because it neither sees him nor knows him. You know him, for he dwells with you and will be in you. (John 14:14-17)

Jesus says another Advocate is going to come. The word he uses for *another* means "another that is just like the first." Jesus is saying the One, the Holy Spirit, would be just like him. Have you ever thought about the significance of having another counselor who is just like Jesus?

Imagine if you could have Jesus Christ standing beside you functioning as your Counselor. Imagine the peace that would bring to your life. Sounds remarkable!

So why do we assume this would be any better than having the literal presence of the Holy Spirit?

When was the last time you saw the Holy Spirit at work in your life? This is where the idea of Christian meditation comes in. It is simply the ability to hear God's voice and obey his word. The truth is the God of the universe desires your nearness. He desires to be close to you. "The wonderful news is that Jesus has not stopped acting or speaking. He is resurrected and at work in our world. He is not idle, nor has he developed laryngitis."[44] Meditation is how we develop closeness with Jesus. It is where we create the emotional and spiritual space for God to meet us in the inward place.

God is always speaking. He is always moving around you. It is ridiculous for us to ask God to "be in this place." The problem is we generally do not always have the eyes to see or the ears to hear. We are always looking for a cosmic voice in perfect Old King James English. When that does not happen, we start to think God must have stopped speaking. Why would Christians claim God has stopped speaking? Did He speak the world into existence? Does matter still exist? Are you still here? Then He is still speaking.

When we are still in meditation, we are depending on God, and we are seeking to think God's thoughts. We desire His presence. We want to know His truth. When did you last set aside time to listen and pay attention to God's truth for your life? Where was the last place you were free from interruption so you could pay attention to what God was saying to your heart?

"For God, who said, 'Let light shine out of darkness,' has shone in our hearts to give the light of the knowledge of the glory of God in the face of Jesus Christ" (2 Cor.

4:6). Regardless of the time, the place, or the posture of your choice, the important thing is that you center your attention, your emotion, your mind, and your spirit on the glory of God in the face of Christ. It can be accomplished in a variety of ways. The primary way is the meditation upon Scripture. It is the internalizing of Scripture. It is not a time of study. You do not analyze the words of someone you love; you accept them as they are uttered to you. This is how meditation works when you read the words of Scripture.

From time to time, take an event in Scripture—a single parable, a couple of verses, or even a single word—and just allow it to take root in your heart.

The Quakers had another form of meditation called centering-down. You make yourself still and silent so you can block out all the distractions and just pray something simple as your heart focuses. Perhaps you pray the Jesus Prayer over and over: "Jesus Christ, Son of God, have mercy on me, a sinner."

You may also meditate on creation. You do not pray or meditate *to* creation. When was the last time you stopped to watch and listen to creation? How you consider creation exposes what you think about the Creator. God is parading His art for you! Do not miss it!

We communicate every day without words. If prayer is communicating, then, sure, words work fine, but so do many other ways. Psalm 46:10 is a verse many Christians know by heart, wherein God tells you to "be still and know that I am God."

It is such a simple verse, but there are two very powerful words we need to understand. Be *still* and *know* are two imperatives. They are commands. What does it mean to be still and know?

For many of us, prayer has the image of sitting perfectly still with our hands crossed at a proper angle in order to really make it work. If any of you have any level of A.D.D., this command to be still is torture. But *rapha*, the Hebrew word for *still* means to sink down and relax. It means to withdraw. Our first command in this verse is to sink down.

Our second command, to know, uses the Hebrew word *yada*. It means to perceive and be acquainted with. We are commanded to sink down, withdraw, and be acquainted with God. This one small and quick verse commands us to perceive and experience God. Could it be that it looks different for everyone? There are several ways to communicate with one another; could there be as many ways to be still and know God?

I once had a conversation with my brother about this. My younger brother is very active and can hardly sit still. He once told me he had connected with the heart of God when he was riding his mountain bike on trails for hours at a time. He said in those times he was able to really disconnect and withdraw from everything else going on and pray. He said he had not felt as close to God as he did on those rides.

Now that makes no sense to me. If I were riding the sort of trails he rode with his level of exertion, I would only be able to think, "Don't die! Don't die! Don't die!" But I am different from him.

One of my former students is a great drummer. He found that he was able to sit down at a full drum set, play for hours, and pray. He could lose time in those moments. Neither does that make sense to me. He is making all sorts of noise, but what's more, his entire body is in motion. I do not have the coordination to play a kazoo, and he said that for the first time in years, he knew his relationship with God was real.

I love writing. I more than love it; I can lose myself in writing. My heart communicates its best in writing. If you give me a pen and paper, I can pour my heart out. I have found myself able to be still in a coffee shop. That makes no sense to a lot of people. "How can you just sit in a noisy coffee shop with all the distractions?" Tonya says she could never do it because she would be distracted by every person who walked through the door. But some of the moments I have felt closest to God were while writing in a coffee shop.

Being still has more to do with the placement of the heart than with the actions of the body. My best friend in high school and I used to go to a little park at very late hours of the night. In this park was a little circle of large boulders. We would both walk in a circle from rock to rock talking out loud about whatever conversation was at hand. I would also go by myself late at night, walk the circle from rock to rock and speak my prayers out loud. I could do this for hours in that place.

You have to find the place where you are still, where you are able to completely withdraw and perceive God in a real and honest place. Find the action that allows you to be still. You may have to be creative. David prayed in a variety of ways. It might be with instruments (Ps. 108) or singing (Ps 13). At times he shouted his prayers (Ps. 20:5). Being still is not a physical action; it is a placement of the heart. It is a placement of that inward place where we can withdraw, relax, and actually forget time enough to connect with God.

Imagine I sat atop a mountain with a sign that said, "I will give you an experience of God for a measly two cents." Do you suppose I would have a great number of people come to me? When you placed a couple of pennies into my bowl, I would give you a couple of grains of sugar. I would ask you to eat it, but do not describe the taste. Do not talk about its sweetness. Just eat the sugar and experience it.

What is sweetness? It could be studied and analyzed in a lab somewhere. You could talk about it sweetness and describe it the very best you can. But the more you talk about sweetness, the less you would know what sweetness is in your own mouth. It is an experience. God is also an experience.

You can talk about God and prove His existence with all the wonderfully orchestrated arguments you can muster, but I agree with Carl Jung on one thing: reality is that which affects you. God is to be experienced, not described and defended. Do you encounter Christ? "You should, you must; for encounter with Christ is the bone and marrow of Christian living. It is the thrilling mystery of grace."[45] Encounter with Christ is not a thing—it is persons who are fused with love encounters.

There are moments when the sweetness is hard to keep from slipping away. We must enjoy spiritual sweetness when it comes and persevere in our relationship with God when it disappears. "In a world obsessed with feelings and experiences, it is easy to assume that spiritual sweetness is one of our inalienable rights."[46] But it is important to remember that this dissolving sweetness happens to those who equate the sweetness of intimacy with emotional comfort.

> Just as the love of a mother for her son can grow deeper when he is far away, just as children can learn to appreciate their parents more when they have left the home, just as lovers can rediscover each other during long periods of absence, so our intimate relationship with God can become deeper and more mature by the purifying experience of his absence.[47]

It is during times like these we can listen closely to our real longings. We can find God in the cries of our longing. In these moments we are able to have an enormous expectation that propels us to intimacy. That patient waiting is the fertile soil of real spiritual growth and maturity.

We have to be careful not to confuse our emotional satisfaction with the presence of God. We are not trying to focus entirely on our own feelings or enjoyment, but we are also not trying to lose the reality of an intimate encounter. Do not come to be more focused on your own feelings than on worshiping Jesus in an intimate encounter. Otherwise, it becomes a fix you have to get. It becomes an obligation just to keep the emotion high. I am not speaking of a Puritan exercise to produce spiritual growth but a heartbeat of your relationship with the One you love. Time with God is not an obligation but a privilege.

The honeymoon is a beautiful tradition in Western marriage. A man and a woman meet each other at the altar, and he vows to love her forever through everything and anything. She thinks, "That is outstanding! Let's go someplace and soak it all up!" Then she vows to love him forever through everything and anything. The man thinks, "For real! I want to celebrate and revel in this; let's go somewhere together and take it all in!" So they do.

When I finally married Tonya, we were able to go on a honeymoon to a location I had kept as a secret from everyone, including her, until the day after our wedding. We went away to Puerto Vallarta and just celebrated our love for each other. We could not stop talking about our wedding and what it meant for our lives. We had professed our love for each other and then we got to just be amazed that this was our life now!

After Jesus was baptized, God said to him, "My beloved, I am so pleased with you. My favor rests on you, my delight is in you." There is a new sort of relationship beginning in this moment. Jesus was discovering God in an incredible new way. Then he went into the desert for what Countinho calls a honeymoon with God, where he was relishing and rejoicing in his relationship with his Father.[48] For forty days he deepened his relationship with God. This is a desperate need we have as those who would encounter God and His love. We need our honeymoon with God.

Can you see Jesus calling you, inviting you, and drawing you? Can you believe that he attracts you and urges you, not from outer space, but from deep inside you? There is a holy nature within you. It is the image of God in you that has its root and life in Christ, and the only way for it to grow is "as the interaction between it and its source is uninterrupted…believe most confidently that Jesus Christ himself delights in maintaining that new nature within you."[49] If you believe this fully enough you can lay aside your self-confidence and rest in the great love of Jesus.

You have an enormous advantage. Moses himself dreamed of something big when he said, "Would that all the Lord's people were prophets, that the Lord would put his Spirit on them!" (Numbers 11:29) What Moses dreamed of is our reality. All followers of Jesus have his Spirit in them and upon them. This is absolutely incredible, but we rarely tap into it, use it, or listen to what Moses only dreamed of.

Several persistent friends have all but demanded that I write a book, and I have always had excuses for why I would not do it. Most of the excuses revolved around not really knowing the right process to actually getting a book published, but I suppose the more exposed reason was I worried whether I was actually capable. I wondered whether I was an adequate writer to produce anything worthy of reading. Do I really have anything sincere enough to offer?

I wrapped myself so tightly in excuses and self-evaluation that I never even considered writing anything. I had evaluated myself out of the ability to move. I often come to the same place with prayer.

I have never considered myself much of a pray-er. I am certainly a far cry from a "prayer-warrior." Though I realize and believe prayer is an open communication with an infinite God, I still find prayer to be far too sparse in my inner journey. Much like writing a book, I often look at prayer and self-analyze out of any movement.

I convince myself that I cannot pray well (if at al) for various excuses. I am not an adequate pray-er. Am I being 100% authentic in prayer if I were to start praying right now? Is it just empty words that will bounce off the ceiling and return to me tauntingly? If I do not pray correctly, would I even know? Do I trust prayer enough to pray? Are my pale attempts really going to connect with such a phenomenal God? Are my prayers too rehearsed? Does God get tired of my redundant ramblings and stale, clichéd prayers? Does He get tired of me closing each sentence with His name? Do I have enough faith when I pray? Do I sound the way I should? I really like the way so-and-so prays; I wish I could pray like that. Do I really care? Am I being weird? Do other people think I am weird? This feels weird. Will God actually respond? When? Soon? Am I doing this right?

I remember a good friend telling me about writing a book. He realized that one just has to start writing. Do not worry about publishing. Do not worry about whether you sound or write perfectly. Just start writing.

The greatest hurdle to prayer is the simple matter of beginning. It is the exertion of your will to start, to act, and move. A chasm of our own crafting separates us from God.

I cannot speak for anyone else, but I know I can excuse, doubt, and self-analyze my way out of movement in most things, and it commonly happens in prayer. I have created a chasm between God and me, and that abyss could be closed if I would just start praying. I need to forget about the questions, the doubts, the wonders, and just *start*! The more I put it off, the more I am trapped in the wondering. Then I get to a point where I am asking myself, "Why don't I pray more often?" Sometimes the only way to begin praying is to do exactly that.

There is something within each of us that wants to grow and mature and develop spiritually. We think all the methods and practices will make us reach the goal. We get focused, but we focus in the wrong direction. Growing in our spiritual lives does not happen by focusing directly on it. Spiritual growth and maturity happens from concentrating on and entangling with the Father.

As a pastor for more than a decade in the machinery of American church, a statement has always vexed me. We like to say there are churches we do not go to because we are not *challenged*. We want to listen to podcasts from speakers who challenge us and we avoid books by authors who do not challenge us. We say we want to be challenged, but I am not sure that is true. We say we want to go to places and people who challenge us, but I think we lie.

To be fair, we lie because we have redefined (falsely) what *challenge* means. When we say we want to be challenged, we mean we want someone to blow our minds. We want someone to communicate something in a way we have never thought about it before. We want to think of things more loftily than we had before. We want to read books that really make us think, and in so doing, make us learn a lot. We want these things, and we call it challenge, but we have misunderstood and forgotten the primary element to challenge.

Action! Movement! Application!

Challenge is a call to engage and change.

We do not really want to be challenged. We want to learn more, maybe. We want to know more information, perhaps. We want to answer more questions correctly than anyone else, probably.

But very few really want to be challenged, because being challenged means being called to the mat where you have to engage and change. Very few of us want to change anything as most of us are too comfortable to change.

Challenge has to do with whether or not you want to engage something enough to enact change in the way you live, act, or do something. Challenge has to do with whether or not what you are reading, hearing, studying, or interacting with engages you to act.

Will life be different? Will I live differently or am I just waiting for you to blow my mind with what you write or say? Do I really want to be challenged, or do I really want to know more information than you? I can think of books I read, and I wonder if any of them, as brilliant as they may be, actually engaged me enough to change, act, or live differently. I think of other books I read in a day or two, but I was engaged to see choices I needed to make to really be closer to Jesus. I can think of some sermons I have heard that rocked my life in a way that made me think, *I really need to change some things!*

The most challenging speakers, writers, and pastors are not necessarily the most profound. This is because it is not their role to be challenging. It is not up to them for you to be challenged. Being challenged is up to you. When presented with something, no matter how simple the presentation, it is up to you to determine whether or not you will engage and change.

The *Queen Mary* was the largest ship to cross the oceans when it was launched in 1936. After four decades and one World War, it was anchored as a floating hotel and museum. While converting into a hotel and museum, the workers took off the massive smokestacks so they could restore them, *but* the smokestacks completely crumbled when they were put on the dock. The workers found that all that was left was about 30 layers of paint and the actual steel stacks had rusted away years before.

For us to find change in all of this, we are going to need to get below the layers we have painted on. "It is the place where I so much want to be, but am so fearful of being. It is the place where I will receive all I desire... but it is also the place where I have to let go of all I most want to hold on to."[50] It is much harder than we realize to engage the heart below our machines.

Jesus shows us the way to respond to all these things. It is done in secret. Our Father God is in that secret place, where no one else is watching or measuring us up. It is in that place where things He cares about and the way He does things begin to transfer to you. "The most strategic thing you can do with your life is to plant it in the secret place with God.... Allow the Lord to meet you in your secret place and develop your roots in hiding. It's important to have a history with the Lord that is hidden, that no one else knows about."[51] He is there waiting for us to go there to listen to Him in solitude. He is waiting to welcome us.

When we are done doing things for other people, our Father who only knows our true self awaits us in the secret place, but we have to get there. God does not see the outward appearance we have created—He only sees the heart and what lies beneath the machinery parts.

We are told our Father who sees in secret will reward us. When we come to that secret place without the influence of everyone around us, we will see more things about ourselves we had not known, but they will be honest because there is no one there to impress or impersonate.

Robert Redford was walking one day through a hotel

lobby, and a woman saw him from across the hall. She caught him just before the door closed on the elevator and asked him, "Are you the *real* Robert Redford?" As the doors closed, he said, "Only when I am alone!"

Soul, I will address you as the Psalmists do. Oh my soul within me, why do you continue to focus on the discouragement, shame, and self-defeat? Why do you not focus on Jesus and the rest He gives to you? (Matthew 11:28-29) Why do you believe the lies of the imposter within you? Listen to the truth of Jesus' words, come to Him, and He will give you rest.

In Jesus, you find your rest. In Jesus, you find rescue and refuge from your troubles. In Jesus, you will find the rest you crave and desire. Oh heart within me, you are under the weight of defeat, and you need rest. Only in Jesus will you find rest from self-defeat, hopelessness, discouragement, and shame. Listen up, soul! You need rest. Only when you are focused on Jesus will you not be focused on the destructive lies and inner dialogue.

Oh my soul, come to Jesus this morning—and tomorrow, and the next day—and you will find rest.

STEP OUT ONTO NOTHING

IN 1999, I was introduced to the writing of Brennan Manning, beginning with most recognized book *The Ragamuffin Gospel.* I swam in the words he wrote because they belted my heart in a way I had never known. When I heard him speak a few times, I was first introduced to the words he used to describe the moment his personal relationship with Jesus Christ began: *When I was first ambushed by the love of Jesus!*

I have yet to discover better words for this stunning reality when Jesus, instead of being a pasty white man with flowing brown hair and Birkenstocks on his feet, becomes authentic, active, and the true loving Lord of a person's life. Ambushed by the love of Jesus was a guttural description of the reality of a heart that beats below the machine parts of my faith up to that point.

There is an unselfconscious freedom in the love of Jesus for you. The heart of Jesus Christ loves you as you are, when you are messed up or broken, beyond shame, limit or remorse, or at rock bottom. In a tattered world like ours, it takes a bit of boldness to believe God's love remains even when your circumstances and choices are destructive.

Isaiah's words still speak to you today, "Be careful,

be quiet, do not fear, and do not let your heart be faint. If you are not in firm faith, you will not be firm at all" (Isaiah 7:4,9). No matter what the world looks like or what is against you, take care and be calm. If you are with God in true intimacy, you do not need to fear and you do not need to be faint of heart. The blunt challenge of verse 9 does not need to be elaborated upon. If you will not believe, you surely will not last.

A donkey finds himself between two equally attractive bales of hay. He stares, hesitates, and stares some more. Eventually he dies because he has no logical justification to move toward one bale or another. Like the donkey torn between two bales, the middle ground is the most dangerous. There is not enough passion to move in any direction.

It is no surprise that many Christians today are beat-down, dried-up, and dilapidated. The world around most Christians has introduced discouragement, cynicism, and a practical atheism that thinks only we can really make things happen. The way we speak and live assumes that God is either dead or in a long sleep. Being ambushed by the love of Jesus does not seem to line up with the things we see in the world. Does it seem to you only a lunatic would believe the heart of God beats for you?

The truth of the gospel does not rise and fall on the headlines and trending stories of your social media. It is not dependent upon the corruption of church leaders, irrational national leaders, or fearmongering media reports. Paul makes it clear that nothing can separate you from the love of Jesus Christ. None of your choices or circumstances can separate you from His love.

If you will disbelieve the gospel and turn your back

on Christianity as a whole, do so because you find the words of Jesus far-fetched, offensive, and saturated with hope. Reject the whole thing if you would like, out of skepticism, turn away from it because you choose a god who is irritable, malicious, or absent, or just waiting for you to flop to smash you, if that really is the sort of god you are choosing. If you cannot accept the idea that God's heart beats for you with expressive love, that is your prerogative. If you do not believe the Father desires you as a friend and lover, then you ought to reject such a ludicrous idea. And if you think it is ridiculous to believe love and hope can triumph over fear and despair, then do not bother with Christianity, because you simply cannot be a Christian unless you do believe that.

Jesus came with an earthshaking message, and it still agitates the foundations of many Christians today. The real Good News is that God pursues and desires you so passionately that you must have a reaction to that love. There must be a point where you are prepared to step out onto nothing, hoping to land on something. There are too few Christians who are willing to exchange everything for the gospel of Jesus Christ. There are even fewer who will fall back into the free-fall of God's enormous love for you. Not many are brave enough.

Are you able to live each day certain that you have been rescued by a matchless grace? After you have fumbled and fallen, are you still convinced that your perfect actions never got you grace in the first place? Are you still shocked to fail? Do you actually believe you do not have to change things to be loved?

Can you overcome doubt and self-defeat with peace and delight? Are you able to walk through days of depression and loneliness with an assurance that joy will be found in the morning? Do other people's perceptions of you or your own false beliefs haunt you? Can you transcend these realities to fully accept the truth that you are loved?

If you cannot, you belong to the brotherhood of broken machines like the rest of us. You may feel like you are dried up and drained out. Can you step out onto nothing today where you sit? Can you determine in this moment to recognize the heart that beats below? That heart beats tirelessly for you, and it is time to be bold.

You can no longer limp through life on your childhood mechanical faith. It is time for making bold decisions, to gamble all you have for the truth of an awaiting love affair. "Imaginative shock issues an invitation which leads to decision and action."[52] If you are truly shocked to know this love is for actually for you, it is time to move. You cannot do nothing.

Jesus came across a paralyzed beggar in John 5, and what did He say to him? This is the most intriguing part of the entire story to me. Jesus came to this guy who had been paralyzed for most of his life, who had come to this pool each day of his life hoping to be healed. Jesus asks him in verse 6, "Do you want to get well?" Could you imagine? Could you imagine what this guy was thinking? *Do I want to get well? Are you kidding me! I have been paralyzed my entire life; what do you think?* It sounds like a crazy question to us, but notice the guy did not answer the question. In fact, his first reaction was to make excuses about why he had not entered the pool yet. It was a yes or no question, and he answered by making excuses for why he simply could not get better. It makes you wonder if he really *did* want to get better or not.

Do we really want to get better? Do we really want our

lives to change? Think about it! We are always talking about being healthier; we want to be fitter, but we never change anything to do that. Maybe we complain about being stuck in a bad relationship we *know* is a bad relationship, but we will not get out of it or do the necessary things to make it better. Perhaps we are stuck in a lifestyle we know we should not be. Perhaps a horrible home life or an unhealthy family dynamic paralyzes us, but we never talk about it with those who care about us. Do we really want to get better? Do we really want things to change?

Usually, it is we who keep us from changing. Even when help or change is possible, we keep ourselves from finding it. Most of the time, we have grown so accustomed to living our lives this way that we are afraid to change. We do not want change because it scares us. We have been trapped for so long that we are used to living this way. We are used to living in this prison of disappointment, misery, pain, helplessness, and failure.

What in your life has you trapped? What do you wish would change? To what are you imprisoned? Do *you* want to change? The same question Jesus gave to the paralytic is given to you today.

Jesus told the man to "Get up! Pick up your mat (or bed) and walk." There were three things Jesus told the man to do, and all three were preposterous things to ask of a paralytic. Could you imagine telling paralytic to *get up, pick up your bed, and walk*?

But Jesus knew this man. Jesus knew what he was asking. Having decided he wanted to change, the man now had to move. Jesus did heal the man, but the paralytic still had to move. He still had to obey Jesus' command.

We generally come to God because we realize, at some point, we are powerless to change our own life. We try so many things to change our own lives, and those things do not work. I came to Jesus when I was tired of trying to fix myself, and I realized I was powerless to change myself. I wanted change. I needed change. I knew something was wrong, but in my own strength I was incapable of changing myself.

There is a common phrase you have likely heard on several occasions. It has become a motto of the world we live in. *You've made your bed; now lie in it.* Each time we make a mistake or bad choice, we hear this phrase. Each time our life gets out of control, we hear this phrase. We have heard it enough times to tell it to ourselves.

It is amazing how the world says one thing and Jesus blows it out of the water. When the world sees your mistakes and your past, it says, "You've made your bed; now you have to lie in it." But when Jesus sees your mistakes alongside your desire to change, he does not say, "You've made your bed; now lie in it." He says, "Get up! Pick up your bed and walk."

What bed are you lying in right now? What are you stuck in? Do you want to get better?

Jesus healed this man not because of who the man was. The man was lazy! He has made excuses his entire life. Jesus healed this man because of who Jesus is. This man did not deserve to be healed. He did not deserve to be loved by Jesus, but because of who Jesus is, this man was healed and loved anyway.

If you have blocked me out this entire book, please listen to me right now. Please hear me say this: God loves you because that it is what God does. God loves you just as you are. He loves you as you are and not as you should be, because you will never be as you should be. God loves you because of who He is, not because of who you are. That is good news! That means you cannot do anything to make God love you more than He already does, and you cannot do anything to make God love you less. His love for you does not depend on you.

Is this the first time you have heard that anyone loves you like that? Have you ever heard about a God who loves you more than anyone will ever love you? Do you want to change? An encounter awaits you.

We have an incredible need for this nearness to God. Especially in light of our incredibly isolated culture, we all but crave a nearness to God. There needs to be a great desire to draw near to God. Do not settle for a Christian life at a distance. Do not be content with a sense of God as a distant thought.

There are a few things we have to understand. First, drawing near to God is not a physical act. We are not building Babel. It is not a church building that draws you near. Drawing near to God is an act of the heart. It is not moving from one place to another. It is directing your heart, an action that happens within us, into the presence of God.

Secondly, remember the reason this is even possible. We trust and know that Jesus Christ came into the world to make a way for this to happen. Christ made a way for us to draw near to God without being held back by things like sin, guilt, and condemnation. You see this throughout the entire New Testament. "For Christ also died for your sins once for all, the just for the unjust, in order that He might bring us to God" (1 Peter 3:18).

"Through Christ we have our access in one Spirit to the Father" (Ephesians 2:18).

This is the center point of the entire Gospel. God has done astonishing and costly things to draw us near to Him. God has done things that appear crazy and unbelievable to us. Think about offering up your own child to die so countless people could actually know *you*. That is crazy! Think about the reality that there is this group of people who are disgusting in comparison to you, but they want to know you and be near to you, so you offer up your child to die in order that they can actually come close to you. It's lunacy!

God does not need us! If we are not there, He is not deprived. But God highlights Himself when He gives us this free gift of access to him. We can actually know God personally and intimately. We can be complete when we come to know Him intimately. God does not need us, but we are an isolated and lonely people who desperately need God!

I have come to know a few things about debt, and many of those lessons have been life lessons for which I have become a better person in the areas of finances. Also, being a student for several years at private Christian universities has also taught me separate lessons about debt. Because of my education loans, I know what it's like to have a debt that seems impossible to escape. I know about an indebtedness that feels much more like a lifelong sentence than a gift of higher education. I know the feeling of debt that is combined and compounded when marrying someone I met at one of those private

Christian universities. For those of you who are doing the math, that is almost 15 years of loan debt.

I also know the sense of believing I will likely die before these are completely paid off. I may literally need to die to pay off these debts.

A few months ago, as I walked on a brisk morning, I tried to imagine the hypothetical euphoria of what it would be like if someone came and paid of all my student loan debt in one written check. I imagined the indebtedness I would feel to that person, but that indebtedness would not be the soul-sucking indebtedness I feel now to my loan provider. No, this indebtedness for a person who paid my debt would be one of exuberant freedom. I would be willing to do whatever I could to serve and honor that person who paid my life-crippling debt.

If someone sacrificed enough of himself to pay off my debt, which may only be paid off when I die, I cannot imagine what I would be willing to do for the life that person gave to my days.

Can you imagine if someone paid off all my debt, and I would not have to live every day of my life with the looming knowledge that I am required to either pay the debt or die? Wow! That really would be good news! I would tell everyone about that person, probably!

My kids are like yours, I assume. They have no troubles asking for things. I have no need to train them in that practice. They have always known how to ask, and sometimes beg, for me to give them things they want and need.

You know what drives me crazy? These kids of mine

do not know gratitude as naturally as they know how to ask. It is embarrassing and irritating that we have to keep telling them to be thankful for things they are given, and once they are grateful we have to teach them to *express* that gratitude.

Our efforts to teach them to be grateful and to say *thank you* seems tireless. It can be irritating to have to ask after they are given something, "Now what do you say?" It is not hard to say thank you, and it does not take that long to express your gratitude. Yet, my children seem to have a hard time being grateful and expressing thanks.

Then God spoke to my heart with a bit of tongue-in-cheek.

"Yeah! It stinks when your children won't take a few minutes to express gratitude and thanks, huh PC?"

Psalm 92 opens with the reminder that "it is good to be thankful to the Lord." Good for what? Good for whom? I am convinced it is good for me to be thankful. I am not so sure it is only good in the sense that a good person is a thankful one. I believe being thankful does me good.

I am thankful for God's grace and mercy on me. Though my heart and soul are distant more often than not, I am always brought back to His grace and love. Though my natural heart resists the pure and Holy Spirit of God to pursue the lies an enemy would want my heart to trust, my cries to God have been heard. He remains close and near. I cannot help but be thankful for these things.

Bernard of Clairvaux spoke about a "perfume compounded of the remembered benefits of God." We can attest to the moments of present blessings, and we are often thankful in the moment. This is one addition to the bouquet of beautiful perfume. But what of the past and the future?

The beauty is in the remembering, not in the benefits or blessings themselves. When we remember with thankful intention, it is a perfume to the Lord. When we fail to remember God's blessings and benefits, we are like something that has died and gone rancid.

Fewer but still some of us will intentionally remember the blessing and benefits of the past when God came through in ways only he could. But what of the future? What about the blessings and benefits yet to be given? What about the promises of God? The promises of God are the blessings and benefits of the future, and we have to be just as thankful and intentional in remembering these.

The beautiful perfume is not a bouquet of benefits and blessings; it is the bouquet of our intentional remembering. Today, stop to remember with gratitude the blessings of your past, present, and future.

The freedom of the gospel, when it ravishes the heart, also enables you to love others differently. If you have really known and experienced the love of Jesus, you are able to tolerate in others what you once found unacceptable in yourself.

The freedom in the gospel of God's love for me is one where I could risk all claims of right or wrong when it comes to actually loving people. If I were questioned for what reason I showed love to a certain person of various character flaws, I see no other response than to say, "I am going to actively love every person, and if I were not supposed to love that person, I trust God will be gracious to me for doing such a terrible thing."

If you really encounter the love and hope found in

the heart of Jesus, nobody needs to hear your tireless words about the gospel. People are hungry for love, hope, security, and courage. They simply look at the way many Christians live and they do not believe us when we talk about love, hope, and security. Nobody needs to believe your words about Jesus if you have not actually experienced and encountered the heart of Jesus.

If I really lived fully confident that God loves me tenderly, I would pour that kind of love out on everyone I was around. If I truly accepted and lived my life with the full understanding of God's unconditional love for me, I could not hold back the healing reconciliation and hope from oozing from my life.

If I truly lived my life in acceptance of God's unending love for me, my only desire would be for everyone to know about it. I would want the only message from my mouth and life to be, "You are loved!"

But many of us do not know that love well enough. Many of us have not truly accepted or believed that love. Many of us attack ourselves and tear ourselves down for myriad reasons, and with each one, deny the fact we are affectionately and deeply loved. We are unable to really accept unconditional love because we hang on to our own conditions. We have a death grip on all the conditions and limits we have placed on love, and in so doing, are incapable of accepting real and true love.

The truth is that unconditional love is available whether I like it or not. I am deeply and warmly loved whether I believe it or not. If I could learn to live in that understanding, it would revolutionize the way I love those around me.

If you grew up around the church for any period of time, you have likely heard the word *passion* frequently used. The word actually means "to be affected by." We are passionate about a great number of things.

I am passionate about Notre Dame football. It affects me, physically. During their games, whether or not I had students over at our home or whether my kids were in sight, I would be cowered in the corner during a game-determining field goal or shouting words to a television I know does not hear me when a game is on the line. Notre Dame football affects me.

While I have a passion for Notre Dame football, that passion may not be as strong as my abhorrence of USC football. It bothers me inside when I see merchandise advertising the University of Southern California. I passionately dislike that team. It affects me.

The great thing about passion is that we choose to allow things to affect us. I allow Notre Dame football and Cubs baseball to affect me, because I am passionate about these things. You are passionate about those things you are most affected by, and that may be just about anything. When I think of the picture of my life and its passions, I want to create a picture of how ridiculous it is to be more passionate about anything other than Jesus Christ and His presence, love, grace, and Spirit.

Does prayer affect me? When I pray, do I come from a place where my heart is affected and affectionate, or are my words without thoughts?

Does my entangled time in God's word affect me? Do I read the things I read wanting to allow myself to actually be affected by what I read, or am I just reading words?

Is my life affected by the love of God today? Not effected, but affected. The former I do not control, the latter I do. Do I allow my heart and life to be affected by the gospel? Am I truly passionate about my closeness to the beating heart of the Father? Does it affect me today? Do I allow his grace to affect my emotion, my choices, and my thirst for *more*?

These are the true questions of passion.

There was a man who wanted to find God. He went knocking on doors asking if anyone knew how he might find God. Someone told him there was a wise sage who lived in the woods. If he went to the sage's house, the sage would help him find God. So he went deep into the woods until he found the man's rickety cabin, and he knocked on the door.

When the sage came to the door, the man said, "It is my understanding that you can help me find God."

The sage paused and looked at him intently. With a stroke his chin, the sage said, "Yes. I can do that. Follow me."

He led the man to a small pond on his property and asked the man to kneel down next to the water and lean over to see himself in the reflection of the still water. As the man knelt down and looked over, the sage took him by the back of the neck and shoved his face under water. He held him there until his whole body jolted in need of air.

The man lifted his head up for a gasp of air, and then the sage shoved his head back under water until he shook violently and nearly drowned before lifting his head back up once more.

The man caught some breath and screamed, "Are you crazy? Are you a lunatic? You told me you were going to help me find God, and here you are trying to kill me!"

The sage looked calmly into the man's eyes and said, "Until you want God as much as you wanted your next breath, you are never going to find Him."

As you stand among the broken and shattered pieces of your life wondering what else God could possibly want with you, do not forget the heart of God that beats beneath your broken machines. His heart is for you. His love is for you. It has always been for you, but until you want the intimate, burning, ridiculous love of Jesus as much as you want your next breath, you may never find it.

NOTES

1. Nouwen, Henri. *Reaching Out: The Three Movements of the Spiritual Life.* (New York: Image Books, 1975), 107.

2. Nouwen, Henri. *The Return of the Prodigal Son: A Story of Homecoming.* (New York: Image Books, 1992), 71.

3. Mumford, Marcus. (2009). White Blank Page. *Sigh No More.* Retrieved from http://www.spotify.com

4. Chambers, Oswald. *My Utmost for His Highest* (Westwood: Barbour and Company, 1935), 333.

5. Manning, Brennan. *The Ragamuffin Gospel.* (Sisters: Multnomah Publishers, 2000), 176.

6. Norris, Kathleen. *Amazing Grace: A Vocabulary of Faith.* (New York: Riverhead Books, 1998), 25.

7. Chan, Francis. *Crazy Love.* (Colorado Springs: David C. Cook, 2008), 66.

8. Vigeveno, H.S. *Letters to Saints and Other Sinners.* (Philadelphia: Holman, 1972), 126.

9. Manning, 30.

10. Shargaa, Jill. (2014, Aug. 29). *Please, Please People. Let's Put the "Awe" Back in Awesome.* Retrieved from Spotify. https://open.spotify.com/episode/4ViJ268h6PHmlHZ7pmnxiw

11. Manning, *The Ragamuffin Gospel*, 102.

12. Countinho, Paul S.J. *How Big Is Your God: The Freedom to Experience the Divine.* (Chicago: Loyola Press, 2007), 6.

13. Countinho, 70.

14. Gray, Donald P. *Jesus, the Way to Freedom.* (Winona: St. Mary's College, 1979), 33.

15. Manning, *The Ragamuffin Gospel*, 78.

16. Countinho, 40.

17. Tozer, A.W. *The Knowledge of the Holy.* (San Francisco: Harper & Row, 1961), 1.

18. Manning, *The Ragamuffin Gospel*, 100.

19. Nouwen, *The Return of the Prodigal Son*, 40.

20. White, E.B. *Charlotte's Web.* (New York: Scholastic, 1952), 114.

21. Manning, Brennan. *Abba's Child: The Cry of the Heart for Intimate Belonging.* (Colorado Springs: Navpress, 2002), 42.

22. Lynch, John, McNicol, B., and Thrall, B. *The Cure: What if God isn't who you think He is and neither are you.* (San Clemente: CrossSection, 2011), 30.

23. Tournier, Paul. *Guilt & Grace: A Psychological Study.* (New York: Harper & Row, 1962), 13.

24. Myers, Glenn. *Seeing Spiritual Intimacy: Journeying Deeper with Mediaeval Women of Faith.* (Downers Grove: IVP, 2011), 128–129.

25. Vigeveno, H.S. *Letters to Saints and Other Sinners.* (Philadelphia: Holeman, 1972), 66.

[26] Manning, *Abba's Child*, 43.

[27] Manning, *The Ragamuffin Gospel*, 175.

[28] Tournier, 20.

[29] Dr. Brand co-wrote a book with Phillip Yancey called *The Gift of Pain*. It is a fascinating read that gets at the connections of physical pain with emotional and spiritual pain, a topic I can only scratch the tip of the surface of here.

[30] Myers, 161.

[31] Gibbons, Dave. *Small Cloud Rising: How Creatives, Dreamers, Poets, And Misfits Are Awakening The Ancient Future Church*. (Irvine: Xealots, 2015), 77.

[32] Ibid., 79.

[33] De Mello, Anthony. *Wellsprings: A Book of Spiritual Exercises*. (New York: Doubleday, 1984), 64.

[34] Nouwen, Henri. *Lifesigns, Intimacy, Fecundity, and Ecstasy in Christian Perspective*. (New York: Doubleday, 1996), 38.

[35] Miller, Donald. *Scary Close*. (Nashville: Thomas Nelson, 2014), 109.

[36] Danforth, John. *The Relevance of Religion*. (New York: Random House, 2015), 34.

[37] Miller, Donald. *Scary Close: Dropping the Act and Finding Intimacy*. (Nashville: Nelson Books, 2014), 124.

[38] Johnston, Ray. *Jesus Called He Wants His Church Back: What Christians and the American Church Are Missing*. (Nashvile: W Publishing, 2015), 24.

[39] Burghardt, Walter. *Grace on Crutches*. (Mahwah: Paulist Press, 1986), 20.

40   Murray, Andrew. *Abiding In Christ*. (Minneapolis: Bethany House, 2003), 114.

41   Tournier, Paul. *Guilt & Grace: A Psychological Study*. (New York: Harper & Row, 1962), 116.

42   Burghardt, 22.

43   Helitzer, Mel. *Comedy Writing Secrets: 2nd Edition*. (Cincinnati: Writer's Digest, 2005), 3.

44   Foster, Richard. *Celebration of Discipline: The Path To Spiritual Growth*. (San Francisco: Harper, 1988), 19.

45   Burghardt, 46.

46   Myers, 107.

47   Nouwen, Henri. *Reaching Out*, 128.

48   Countinho, 69.

49   Murray, 61.

50   Nouwen, *The Return of the Prodigal Son*, 13.

51   Liebscher, Banning. *Rooted: The Hidden Places Where God Develops You*. (Colorado Springs: Waterbrook, 2016), 107.

52   Shea, John. *Stories of God*. (Chicago: Thomas More Press, 1978), 187.

Made in the USA
San Bernardino, CA
04 December 2016